COMING TO
A Theology of Beauty

COMING TO

A Theology of Beauty

by WILLIAM D. DEAN

BL
65
. A4
D4

THE WESTMINSTER PRESS

Philadelphia

ISBN 0-664-20932-7 (cloth)

ISBN 0-664-24950-7 (paper)

LIBRARY OF CONGRESS CATALOG CARD No. 71-181723

BOOK DESIGN BY
DOROTHY ALDEN SMITH

Published by The Westminster Press ®
Philadelphia, Pennsylvania

PRINTED IN THE UNITED STATES OF AMERICA

To Patty,
who transmits a confounding beauty

CONTENTS

CONTENTS

PREFACE

This is no call to come to and tie up in one of the safe harbors of the religious mainland. In those harbors are offered the unchanging Word, the ongoing Forgiveness and the primal Mystery. But the prospect for significant transaction in such goods seems to be diminishing.

This is a call to come to an understanding of the meaning of the voyage. In particular ways it appeals for a coming to. It appeals for a shaking of the head, a coming to from recurring dreams of Truth, Morality, and the Holy. And it appeals for a more positive coming to: a dawning sense of appreciation, an appreciation expressed in wonder and celebration, but an appreciation divested of a carefree naïveté.

It is an appreciation provoked by what is coming to man: the new possibilities which come, unexpectedly. Testimony to such novelty is found in the simple experience of serendipity, as well as in the discovery of a "pretty" model of the double helix by J. D. Watson, as well as in realizations of new forms of love.

It is an appreciation that is best called aesthetic. When the novelty that comes is related to the world that is, beauty is experienced.

This appreciation presupposes a world where the passage is guided by the prevailing winds rather than by the demands of the harbors. Reality is processive, rather than static. It is coming to be, rather than standing still. Time erodes the directives from the past harbors and obscures the signals from future harbors. Remaining are the floating clouds, the drifting stars, the swirling sea. Present experience is left. The voyage is the goal. But then what provides an orientation? On uncharted waters, with no fixed points out of the past or future, where is value found? What meaning there is must be in the eventfulness of the passage, must be made possible by the novelties which come on the way, and must be felt as aesthetic experience.

We claim to be doing theology. And the excuse for that claim is the apparent impossibility of explaining how novelty is presented to the wondering individual apart from some conjecture that it comes to man from God. This last sense of coming to is intellectually embarrassing. But, then, intellect—in its academic use—is usually too susceptible to embarrassment.

The concluding chapter is a small effort to counter the rude treatment given aesthetics in Western religious thought. It is an effort to go on to spell out some theological and religious implications of a certain perspective on God, one that concentrates, not on God as Truth, or as Goodness, or as the Holy, but on God as beautiful.

Sometimes it is a pleasure to announce dependencies. I think of those who in recent years were for me living illustrations of an aesthetic mode of life—like Pat Kelly, a sculptor in Nova Scotia, and Tom Ortman, a farmer and railroadman in Ashland, Wisconsin. I think of teachers at the University of Chicago to whose track I switched —like Bernard Meland and Bernard Loomer—and of those who were patient enough to keep flashing the caution light to show the perils ahead—like Langdon Gilkey and Joseph Sittler. I think of those who read and criticized this manuscript—like Keith Keeling, Bryant Keeling, and, most especially, Lawrence Owen. I think of my secretary, Jan Nelson, who kept things in repair, and of the Gustavus Research Fund, which kept the skids greased. I wrote with some idea of my cynical siblings looking over one shoulder, my trusting parents looking over the other shoulder, and my expectant children at my feet. But the woman whose husband I am actually sat across the table and said, No! Again, no. Try it this way. It should be better. Sentence by sentence, on into the night. And she was almost always right.

I hold none of these people responsible. But, then, I think the average reader would know that I could not, even if wanted to.

W.D.D.

COMING TO
A Theology of Beauty

CHAPTER I

SOMETHING NEW

If you like to think that progress in an academic discipline is a steady building, broader and higher, block upon block, then for theology the 1960's were disastrous. Much was destroyed or at least called seriously into question. Little of apparent permanence was added. There must be decades like that in every discipline. But whereas a theologian in 1960 was preoccupied with problems of conveying what seemed to be settled truths, a theologian in 1970 was preoccupied with justifying to himself the legitimacy of his own profession.

A theologian is ill-fitted for other work, so he is inclined to be optimistic even when the odds are deplorable. He is often toughened by defeat. He witnessed an all-out and generally successful attack on neo-orthodoxy and he had to remind himself one day that the mainstay of neo-orthodoxy—existentialism—was no longer much discussed. A pleasant retreat to an old, rationalistic, optimistic liberalism was blocked not only by the lingering effects of neo-orthodoxy and existentialism, not only by the cen-

tury's schooling in man's inhumanity, but also by strictures from philosophy—especially, that movement in philosophy known as linguistic analysis. Yet, while linguistic analysis frowned on the use of speculative reason in
theology, even in the more updated versions of theology,
such as Paul Tillich's or the theologies informed by process thought, linguistic analysis seems to have contributed
little of constructive merit in theology. To add insult to
injury, even the "death of God" school of theology,
which seemed prepared to accept all this and go on, soon
lost a hearing; the death of the "death of God" theology
was accepted about as rapidly as the "death of God"
theology accepted the "death of God." But as they looked
back over the smoking ruins, some thought that they de-
tected a new odor—perhaps caused down deep by a new
combustion of old elements flowing together to form
new compounds.

We will spare the reader a survey of olfactory sensations
on the edge of a theological dump. But we would encourage him to sample and analyze one specimen. It can
be done in an easy chair between the antiseptic covers
of a small book.

I

In the waning months of the '60s, religious book
publishing gave us what may prove to have been a
preview of some of the themes that will occupy
theological writing in the '70s: wonder, celebration,
comedy and play. Though at first sight appearing—
particularly in view of the monumental urban, racial

and international crises of the hour—to be heralding a most unlikely and untimely revival of A *Child's Garden of Verses*, *Alice in Wonderland* and *Huckleberry Finn*, these four closely interrelated themes may turn out to be if not the dominant notes at least the grace notes that will characterize theological compositions in the coming decade.[1]

M. Conrad Hyers wrote this in a review of Robert E. Neale's *In Praise of Play*, and he went on to cite other books, all published in 1969, which might be included in this trend: Harvey Cox's *Feast of Fools*, Sam Keen's *Apology for Wonder*, David Miller's *Gods and Games*, and his own *Holy Laughter*. Apparently these books are included in this trend because they use such words as "wonder," "celebration," "comedy," and "play." Hyers does not explicitly state how these words are themes rather than simply earmarks of something deeper, nor does he say how these themes are interrelated. But Hyers was short on space. Besides, sometimes it takes more faith to accept writings on religion than to accept those realities which religion is about. So let us take Hyers on faith. There are several interrelated themes in the books and together they indicate something new to come in theological writing in the 1970's. We venture the hope that these themes might amount to more than theological "grace notes." Perhaps they can be "dominant notes" for people suffering from religious confusion.

So, with such faith and hope, let us examine these books in the ensuing pages of this chapter. We will describe and analyze their contents and outline how it seems that they might be sounding, from different angles, a little-known terrain in the theological depths.

(We will alter Hyers' list of books, however, by excluding his own *Holy Laughter*, because it is really an anthology of essays, dating from 1946 to 1967, which does not incorporate the innovative motifs present in the recently written books. And we will add Sam Keen's *To a Dancing God* because this book supplements Keen's *Apology for Wonder*.)

HARVEY COX
The Feast of Fools: A Theological Essay on Festivity and Fantasy
Harvard University Press, 1969. 204 pp.
Paper edition: Harper & Row, Publishers, Inc., Colophon Books, 1971

Initial reactions, just after purchase:

Assumption: When Harvey Cox raises his finger, sometimes the wind blows so that he can test it.

Question: Has this happened again? Or were there already new winds of doctrine boiling over the horizon?

The book: The pages glisten as Harvey Cox walks on them.

Subtitle: A Theological Essay on Festivity and Fantasy.

Paradigm: The medieval Feast of Fools (Jan. 1), when "pious priests and serious townfolk donned bawdy masks, sang outrageous ditties, and generally kept the world awake with revelry and satire," and when "no custom or convention was immune to ridicule and even the highest personages of the realm could expect to be lampooned." [2]

Thesis: The sense of fantasy and the spirit of festivity should be reinfused into our individual lives, our society, and our religious thought and activity.

A *more deliberate analysis*, a few days later:

Man is by nature a creature who can celebrate and who can envision hypothetical situations. He can be festive and he can be fanciful. There are indications that these capacities are withering. Man as an individual suffers from this loss, for he is abusing capacities that distinguish him from other creatures and that by their sheer exercise improve life. The human species and human society suffer from this loss, for apart from festivity and fantasy, adaptation and social innovation perish. Man as a religious being suffers from this loss, for religion depends on a sense of a larger cosmic and historic context, and without festivity and fantasy this sense atrophies.

Festivity is celebrative activity that contrasts with ordinary life in that it is excessive and also qualitatively different from everyday happenings. By definition it has a holiday spirit. The waning of the spirit of festivity in the Western world has meant that man has become confined to the narrowest sense of history, history that is limited to technological, rational, manipulated, work-oriented ordinariness. Man has lost that broader history, which is the cosmic context in which ordinary history has traditionally been set. Cox argues that this is the explanation for the "death of God" phenomenon: man in fact is expressing his own inability to contact realities beyond those typical of mundane history. And Cox argues that a restoration of a spirit of festivity would place man again in the broader framework within which mundane history should be set. For festivity is not simply excessive and extraordinary activity; it is also activity *about* that which is extraordinary.

> Celebration, in short, reminds us that there is a side of our existence that is not absorbed in history-making, and therefore that history is not the exclusive or final horizon of life.[3]

If festivity is participation in a broader context through activity, fantasy is participation in a broader context through "envisionment." It is the capacity to entertain imagined possibilities; and in doing so, rules are suspended and structures may be broken. But in our hard-nosed, problem-solving culture there is a deep suspicion of fantasy. Fantasy is neglected as a means of inquiry. Cox explains ways in which fantasy might be restored. He suggests that the church should foster the use of fantasy and that it should serve as a channel for introducing the creations of fantasy into society. But, whether by the church or by other groups, fantasy's resources must be brought into the service of re-creating the world.

Near the end of *The Feast of Fools* Cox offers a few suggestions on more conventional theological topics: method and Christology. He proposes a method of juxtaposition that would capitalize on the advantages of festivity and fantasy. Festivity and fantasy are of distinctive epistemological value because they prompt the individual to back off from practical preoccupations and to grasp broader and more subtle dimensions of reality. When theology neglects festivity and fantasy, it falls victim to restricted preoccupations. The Traditional Christian thought concentrates excessively on the past, the "death of God" theology concentrates excessively on the present, and the theology of hope concentrates excessively on the future. Cox maintains that, in theology, if the past, the present, and the future were considered simultaneously—with a full recognition of the discontinuities and conflicts that would arise from such juxtaposition—then a more balanced, vital, and imaginative approach to theology might become possible. Cox suggests that a comic style can incorporate this juxtaposition.

Accordingly, he entitles his concluding chapter, "Christ the Harlequin." He reasons that in our time a tragic acceptance of a negative fate is inappropriate; similarly, a progressivistic optimism is inappropriate. We are simultaneously imbued with doubts and fascination, disillusionment and hope. A Christology of the harlequinesque, juxtaposing the negative and the positive, can provide the comic perspective that is germane to festivity and fascination, that is appropriate to our time, and that can still preserve a germ of hope. Cox develops the theme by discussing prayer as play, and by reviewing recent literature that concentrates on the comic dimension in Christianity.

This concluding chapter is apparently the keystone of the book. It speaks more specifically of how Christianity can interpret and utilize festivity and fantasy. Christ the harlequin is apparently the prime instance of the method of juxtaposition, which calls for a focusing "precisely on those discomfiting points where memory, hope, and experience contradict and challenge each other." [4] Yet it is strange that when Cox seeks the quintessential instance of the vitality that comes from the juxtaposition of the past, present, and future, he turns quite unselfconsciously to the Christ of the past. Now it could be argued that Cox is dealing with "the Christ" generically, as the timeless *logos* manifested in brand-new forms; for Cox does talk of Christ the harlequin's "unexpected entrance onto the stage of modern secular life." [5] But, if this is the case, why does he attempt to speak of the New Testament Christ, the Christ of the past, as the source of "clown symbols"? [6] Or why does Cox not indulge in some of the "discomfiting" contrasts between what could be really different Christs of the past, present, and future? This is all confusing. For it seems that Cox unfurls a fresh new banner, but then runs it up the old pole. Cox offers a radical new substance, but then we are asked just to take the same old wine from a new skin. The question is, Has Cox brought his notion of revelation, and in particular his idea of Christ, into the swim? Or does it stand, winking from the shore like an old beacon?

Cox has written a fresh and insightful study. He has not claimed to have written a rounded theological exposition, and he leaves unanswered some basic questions. He does not say how, epistemologically, the fresh data of festivity or fantasy enter experience. He does not say how or why God would promote festivity or fantasy. And he does not say how man is such that he can relate festivity and fantasy to truth, to ethics, or to classical accounts of the experience of the holy.

David L. Miller
Gods and Games: Toward a Theology of Play
The World Publishing Company, 1969. 206 pp.

On finishing this book you might have the feeling that
David Miller had a good article in mind and then someone talked him into writing a book. For Miller's distinctive notion of the relation between play and religion
is preceded by a huge encyclopedic cataloging of almost
everybody's notions of play.

Miller argues that every culture is ordered around a
meaning system, or mythology, which is anchored in a
root metaphor. Western culture is in the midst of a
mythological revolution, from a work- or doing-centered
mythology to a play mythology. Miller says: "It may well
be that we are becoming accustomed to viewing all things
sub specie ludi. Play is our *mythos*. Play is a metaphor
of contemporary meaning." [7] While he offers descriptions
of other theories of play, Miller never seems to get around
to proffering his theoretical definition of play. But he
does give four functions of the play mythology: (1) *aisthesis*, the spiritual function, whereby all the senses are open
to the wonder of being; (2) *poiesis*, the natural-cosmic
function, in which it is recognized that reality must be
comprehended by a fictional order, rather than a literal
order; (3) *metamorphosis*, the social-coherence function,
in which it is seen that change is the only consistent form
of social order; and (4) *therapeia*, the psychological function, where a purposeless waiting for meaning is the highest form of personal organization.

Miller concludes, through a strange bit of reasoning, that the play mythology has religious importance:

> The famous scholar of religions Joachim Wach once said that "the primary theoretical expression of the religious experience is myth." Thus [sic], to the extent that the meaning-system whose root metaphor is play is vital in our time, to that extent play is not only man's myth but also his religion.[8]

Miller goes on to note that the four functions of the play mythology are religious in that they concern man ultimately; they involve faith.

A theology for a religion of play is a theology of play. The form of such a theology must be consistent with its content. Miller concludes that the form of a theology of play should be aphoristic. An aphorism embodies fundamental ambiguity; it is like a definition that is open-ended, a joke whose punch line is hidden.

The faith behind a theology of play is described as "make-believe." While aphorism is the theological form of a religion of play, faith is the religious form of a religion of play. And the form of religion must be consistent with its play content. Faith as make-believe is

> being turned on by an incredible vision. . . . It is playing as if it were true. It is not that the religious story is not true. It is simply that questions of truth are irrelevant while in the midst of make-believe, while in the midst of faith.[9]

This approach contrasts with belief, which, as Miller uses the word, is the work attitude that attempts to trade an assertion about the truth of something for a payoff of some kind. Belief in this sense is magical: if you believe something, then you can control something that is not normally subject to human control. But faith as make-believe also contrasts with profane nonbelief.[10] Faith is the play of having confidence, without concern for truth —especially in the sense that truth has to do with manip-ulation.

This, then, is the essence of Miller's own notion of the relation of play to religion. As we indicated earlier, the remainder of the book is a catalog of other theories of play. However, this raises a curious question.

Miller has said that a theology of play should be aphoristic if it is to have a form consistent with its con-tent. But Miller is himself writing a theology of play; the subtitle of his book is *Toward a Theology of Play*. Hence, the book itself must be aphoristic. And Miller is quite self-conscious about this:

> If this book becomes a bit playful at the end, it will be because the hobby horse (about "play" as a new mythology) is being as well fed and as pas-sionately cared for as Earnest Calkins'. [11]

> But lest the reader think this is only a play with words and is losing the fun of it, we had better turn the page and begin seriously.[12]

> If at times the account seems a bit fanciful or play-ful, the reader would do well to remember that, like all history, this is the author's story.[13]

> If a book purports to witness to life lived *sub specie ludi*, perhaps then there should not be a serious word in the whole book. . . . I seriously hope that

there is not one serious sentence in the whole of
this book. Including this last one.[14]

Now with all this the reader can wonder if there is any
breathing space left for the ostensible aphoristic ambiguity of a theology of play. Consequently, the idea of the
congruity between a play content and a play form, which
could have been Miller's most significant contribution
to the discussion, suffers in application. Nevertheless,
Miller, especially in the "Introduction" and the "Epilogue," makes a valiant attempt to embody an aphoristic style. The "Epilogue," which Miller refers to as a
"theology made up of play" or a "playful theology," is a
series of gnomic paradoxes and quotations that are un-
systematically strung together and can render an amusing effect.

Unwittingly (or, wittingly?) Miller has made his catalog of theories of play, which comprises over two thirds
of the book, the most ironic and amusing part of the
book. For set in this volume, which is ostensibly laced
with a playful form, is a great swelling corpus of earnest
scholasticism. Ch. 2, "The Contemporary Academic
Game of Games" (pp. 17–94), is a description of past
theories of play. The survey is accomplished through discussions of the following individuals, each of whose
names is introduced by being placed in capitals: Johan
Huizinga, Joseph Campbell, Adolf Jensen, Roger Callois,
George Herbert Mead, Talcott Parsons, Erving Goffman,
Peter Berger, Nigel Calder, "Adam Smith," Stephen Pot-
ter, Edouard Claparede, Harvey C. Lehman, Paul A.
Witty, Jean Piaget, Arnold R. Beisser, Eric Berne, A. H.

Chapman, Thomas Szaz, Gregory Bateson, Don Jackson, Jay Haley, John Weakland, Franz Alexander, Norman O. Brown, Herbert Marcuse, Erik Erikson, Sigmund Freud, John Ciardi, Thomas Mann, W. H. Auden, Luigi Pirandello, Rainer Maria Rilke, Hermann Hesse, Jean Genet, Tom Stoppard, Karl A. Olsson, Edward Albee, Julio Cortazar, Samuel Beckett, Josef Pieper, Ludwig Wittgenstein, Hans-Georg Gadamer, Eugen Fink, Friedrich J. J. Buytendijk, Theodor Haecker, Robert S. Deropp, Alan Watts, Dom Aelred Graham, Father Hugo Rahner, Robert Lee, Eleanor Shelton Morrison, Robert E. Neale, Gerardus Van der Leeuw, and Sister Mary Corita. Many other authors, not honored with capitals, are cited. And play theories in the following academic areas are discussed: anthropology, ethnology, sociology, economics, psychology, literary criticism, literature, philosophy, mathematics, and theology. And ninety-two footnotes are listed. This is real scholasticism, for there is no real theoretical framework other than the academic areas and the fact that all the authors mention play. The citation of data is sufficient unto itself. The next two chapters discuss the origin and history of play in the world of thought and in the development of the individual. There is an earnest argument here: culture has proceeded from an original sense of playfulness, to a work orientation (which lasted twenty-five centuries), to a maturation to a renewed playfulness (which is just now, of course, coming into full view). Correspondingly, an individual is born into a sense of infantile playfulness, learns to work, and finally returns to playfulness.

Miller has done a study and added some of his own conclusions. As in the case of Cox, he does not say how, epistemologically, play is possible or significant. He does not say how or why God would promote play. He does not say how man is such that he can relate play to truth or ethics, or how, in detail, play is related to classical accounts of the experience of the holy.

ROBERT E. NEALE
In Praise of Play: Toward a Psychology of Religion
Harper & Row, Publishers, Inc., 1969. 187 pp.

Since the question of the relation of the form to the content of an exposition about play has been broached already, it might be worth seeing what Neale has to say about it:

> It is difficult for modern man to write and read about play in the appropriate spirit, that is, play-fully.[15]

> It should be anticipated that the author's vision of play will be veiled by implicit praise of work. Every theory of play under consideration exhibits this bias, and it would be unrealistic to assume that the author is somehow able to escape the presupposition of his society. The vision of play will be partial and corrupt.[16]

> Our essay has only been an essay in praise of play. But the author may well be as much a worker as anyone else.[17]

Neale's prose is studious; so, while these comments are commendably humble, they also seem accurate.

The content of Neale's theory of play is predominantly psychological. It is informed by J. C. Friedrich von Schiller. Man has a dualistic nature: he has the need to discharge energy and the need to design experience. The need to discharge psychic energy orients the individual toward the moment in time, the object in space, the specific, however it is. The need to design and organize experience orients the individual toward the permanent, the universal, and the formal. These two needs are basic to any individual; but they can be related in conflict or in harmony. When they are related in conflict, one dominates the individual and the other is neglected. If discharge rules, the individual is ruled by the accidental and the random; if design rules, the individual is ruled by the general and the abstract. Discharge can bring immediate pleasure, but can destroy the order to life; design can bring order, but destroy experience of immediacies. Where these needs are in conflict, there is the psychological condition called work: "Work is the attempt to resolve inner conflict." [18] The individual enduring a battle for dominance between the two aspects, suffers from internal attrition: sheer psychic energy, properly expended in outward activities, is dissipated in the internal battle with the ordering side of the self; a sense of orientation, properly expended in ordering the world beyond the self, is curtailed by the battle with the unruly discharging side of the self. Work is the activity directed toward resolving this destructive conflict, using whatever energy and orientation remain after this internal attrition. Usually, the individual fails to discern that the problem is with himself, and he projects his problems on the world.

So he goes out, ostensibly to resolve the conflicts of the external world. But the truth is that this individual is selfishly using the world as a battleground for the resolution of his internal problems. This is true despite the fact that a work-oriented world honors him as responsible and altruistic.

Where the discharge of energy and the design of experience stay within limits and coexist in harmony, there is play. While work is the attempt to resolve inner conflict, "play is any activity not motivated by the need to resolve inner conflict." [19] The player can bring his full energies and designing capacities into the world and operate with genuine compassion.

Now these definitions of work and play are ideal. No individual exists in a state of perfect conflict or perfect harmony. Nevertheless, they define a spectrum wherein activities can be seen as more work-oriented or more play-oriented. Also, it should be clear that any given activity can be work or play. What counts is the psychological source of the activity.

Neale goes on to fill in his abstract definition of play with a phenomenology of play. Play is an adventure in that it involves chance, risk, and importance. And as adventure it includes the elements of peace, freedom, delight, and illusion, and it proceeds under the modes of story and game.

Neale devotes the remainder of the book to a discussion of the relation of play to religion. He does not relate play and religion as separate entities. Instead he relates the two by arguing that religion is something within play;

religion can be subsumed under the psychology of play.

Psychic conflict and the work reaction to it comprise the realm of the profane. Psychic harmony can eventuate either in magic or religion. When the individual is freed from psychic conflict, his discharge of energy and design of experience exist in harmony and are released for creative expression beyond the self. This new discharge of energy and design of experience give to the individual "powerful form": power relating to the discharge and form relating to the design. This powerful form *is* the sacred: "The sacred is the realm of new discharge and new design." [20] "The sacred is always manifest as form as well as power; awareness of the sacred is awareness of powerful form." [21] Religion is the playful response to powerful form. Religion is full play, where full play is the utilization of the new discharge and design in the absence of internal or external conflicts.

The two modes of play, story and game, are seen in religion as myth and ritual.

To assess Neale's book is difficult. Certainly this psychology of play generates a fresh and intriguing definition of religion. One is not left with the suspicion, as one might be with Cox's book, that many of the old orthodox Christian verities have been merely realigned, rather than radically reconceived. One is not left with the suspicion, as one might be with Miller's book, that this is primarily a catalog of other theories of play, with a trailing appendage added by the author. The book is not even explicitly Christian,[22] and the author's theories dominate the whole work.

Neale treats religious language in a way analogous to the way Paul van Buren treats religious language in *The Secular Meaning of the Gospel*. In both books the only religious language that is meaningful is that which functions within the academic discipline of the author—within linguistic analysis for van Buren and within psychology for Neale. In both books there is no place for a God who is active or is real beyond man. Van Buren thus drops the use of the word "God." Neale uses the word "God" to refer to the new release of energy and design *within* the human psyche. Religious terms, such as faith and myth, have no vector from man to a reality beyond man; they refer to human acts. For Neale, faith [23] is simply participation in a kind of mythical expression, and myth arises out of the harmony of psychic discharge and design.[24] The greatest difference in the approach of van Buren's book and Neale's is that van Buren makes a great deal of the "secular" radicalness of his new interpretation, while Neale never refers to his interpretation in this way.

Neale is working within the closed world of human psychic events. How then does he refer to the discharge and design as "new," unless by new he means, not that there is an incursion of potentials from beyond man, but that there is simply a new release of innate human capacities from the jam of psychic conflict? How does he find it appropriate to relate his own notion of the sacred with Mircea Eliade's and Rudolf Otto's,[25] and hence talk of it as fascinating and repelling, if in fact the sacred is simply the coming to fruition of normal human capacities? In short, does play introduce to human culture genuinely fresh possibilities, or is it simply the maturation of a static human nature, which is the same through time immemorial? Without the participation of a God who is more than man, how can fresh possibilities arise? We are arguing that Neale not only does not make explicit a metaphysical dimension, he rejects it. It is possible that in this view play becomes simply a sign of psychic health, rather than a source of major innovation.

Finally, Neale does not offer any detailed explanation of the relation of play to truth or goodness.

SAM KEEN
Apology for Wonder
Harper & Row, Publishers, Inc., 1969. 218 pp.

SAM KEEN
To a Dancing God
Harper & Row, Publishers, Inc., 1970. 160 pp.

In the coffee shop recently, a friend of mine said that the earlier book was just old study notes and that the latter book went ahead and did it. The titles themselves might bear this out: Keen moves from *apologia* to salutation, from theory to something closer to an account of practice. Better yet, there is a change in the covers— from a big picture of Sam Keen's naked face on the first, to orange ladies dancing naked on the second. (The irony here is that somebody had the effrontery to charge three times as much for the first one.)

Apology for Wonder is not a one-sided advocacy of wonder. Keen's general apology is for the timely man, *homo tempestivus:* man who at the right times adopts, in turn, the best aspects of both *homo faber* (manipulating man) and *homo admirans* (wondering man). The particular problem addressed in the book is that contemporary views of man neglect that side of man which includes his capacity to wonder. Consequently, modern man has become the manipulative *homo faber;* the image of man as a receptive *homo admirans* has been nullified.

The first two chapters of *Apology for Wonder* describe the characteristics of wonder and the exemplification of wonder in childhood experience. Keen then places wonder in historical perspective. It is the traditional man who best exemplifies the sense of wonder. The traditional man—whether primitive man, the man of classical Greece, or the man of Biblical places and times—understood the cosmos as unified and meaningful; he interpreted his life and environment as a gift; and he was motivated to emulate that cosmic meaning. There were differences between the three types of traditional man: while primitive man and Greek man saw the world-ordering mind as immanent and as apparent in nature, the Judeo-Christian man saw that mind as transcendent and as apparent in history. However, they were united in believing that the meaning of the cosmos was given to them and that they should be receptive to this given meaning. To be receptive was to be open and sensitive to the meaning that came. It was to wonder. Traditional man was wondering man: *homo admirans.*

What happened to that unified and meaningful cosmos

of old has been told before, and it is retold by Sam Keen. Ontological reason, which once discerned a meaningful cosmos, was attacked and replaced by a technique of calculating reasoning and a sense of the historical limitedness of reason. The order of a universe was replaced by the contingency of a multiverse. And a new sense of evil and talk of the death of God arose. The cosmos came to appear chaotic. So man alone was left to create meaning. Receptivity became pointless. Wonder was buried and paved over by an aggressive, active, manipulating *homo faber*. Modern man has attempted to make his world by himself.

Keen then subsumes the two images of man under two classical representations of the authentic life. *Homo admirans* is viewed in terms of the Dionysian mode of life; *homo faber* is viewed in terms of the Apollonian mode of life. Keen argues that either mode of life by itself leads to "ideopathologies." The Apollonian mode at the extreme chokes off the freedom and wonder of possibility for the sake of what is felt to be necessity. The Dionysian mode at the extreme succumbs to the vacuousness of total possibility and ignores the necessities and limits that govern life.

> *Homo admirans* accepted the world as a gift and affirmed that the highest and most appropriate human act was contemplation and celebration; however, he refused to assume full responsibility for remaking the world closer to the heart's desire. . . . *Homo faber* has abandoned the notion of the impious and has assumed total responsibility for molding the chaos of nature into the secular city, but in

so doing has lost the ability to celebrate anything other than the products of his own hands.[26]

Hence, Keen reaches the not very startling conclusion that authentic man must reject an exclusive alliance to either mode of life and accept appropriate advantages of both modes. Man must do this according to a temporal model, pursuing the Apollonian way when that is appropriate and the Dionysian way when that is appropriate. Man must become *homo tempestivus*.

As Cox did, Keen concludes by repurchasing a few conventional theological terms with the new coinage minted in the course of the book. He defines grace as trust in the world (in the spirit of *homo admirans*) combined with confidence in the self's ability to take appropriate action (in the spirit of *homo faber*). For the religious person, trust is founded on a belief in some "ground of being"; for the nonreligious person, trust is at least the affirmation that what is not controlled by *homo faber* is not sinister. Gratitude is expressed as worship or celebration. Gratitude for the religious person is worship, from the given world to the giving God. For the nonreligious person, it is celebration, where *"celebration consists of rejoicing in the presence of things* rather than going beyond them." [27]

How important is it to know the name of the stranger and thank him for his gift? . . . Whether we continue to talk about God is not so important as whether we retain the sense of wonder which keeps us aware that ours is a holy place.[28]

To a Dancing God was published in the year following the publication of *Apology for Wonder*. A summary
description of the content of *To a Dancing God* is about
as pointless as a summary description of someone's collection of short stories. For the book is a collection of essays
on a number of questions and topics. However, as with
a collection of short stories, it is possible to comment
in a general way on perspectives and themes that perme-
ate most of the pieces.

A paragraph in the "Introduction" indicates the movement that came between *Apology for Wonder* and *To a
Dancing God:*

> The dancing god to whom the title of this book
> refers is neither Apollo nor Dionysus. Indeed, he is
> nameless and, perhaps, must remain so. My (our?)
> only assurance is that he inhabits me (us?) as often
> in discipline as in spontaneity, as much in decision as
> in ecstasy, as frequently in promises as in immedi-
> acy. As always, the sacred shatters all the categories
> we necessarily use to understand the sacred. So
> the dance continues. That is life. And for it I wish
> to offer these libations.[29]

The Apollonian and Dionysian categories are blurred. In
Apology for Wonder, Keen allows for the possibility
of a named God; here God has become simply name-
less. Even the presumption of the scholarly plural is
placed in question, in favor of the more modest and
personal first person singular. Yet the signal emphasis on
spontaneity, ecstasy, and immediacy remains, although
the emphasis has moved from a more contemplative and

intellectual "wonder" to a more vital and physical "dance."

While in *Apology for Wonder* Keen is reacting against the predominance of the *homo faber* mentality of contemporary man, in *To a Dancing God* he is reacting against the predominance of tradition, whether religious, educational, revelational, or Apollonian. He discusses religious time (Ch. 1, "Exile and Homecoming"), or the need to overcome the tyranny of past traditions and to live in the present and the future as well as the living past; education (Ch. 2, "Education for Serendipity"), or the need to incorporate wonder and carnality into education; revelation (Ch. 3, "Reflections on a Peach-Seed Monkey or Storytelling and the Death of God"), or the need to recognize that, while the traditional stories may be dead, there remain the personal stories with their ability to open spiritual depths; and personal reflections in a Dionysian vein (Ch. 4, "Diary of a Jubilee Year").

Keen's inductive exploration does issue in a few summary comments in the closing chapter, "The Importance of Being Carnal—Notes for a Visceral Theology." Keen is sick of Christianity's insistence that salvation comes from the memory of ancient events mediated through words by an authoritative church. Keen expresses the point aptly:

> Characteristically, Protestantism has declared that healing comes not from what may be seen, or felt, or touched but from *hearing* the word of God. The ear is the organ of salvation. . . . Unless we are able to locate the presence of that which heals and

saves in *contemporary history*, on the soil of what is immediately experienceable, unless we are able to get away from the idea that obedience (intellectual or moral) to some external authority that testified to having heard THE WORD is the prerequisite for healing, we will not be able to understand that grace which comes from the viscera and which is available wherever beauty or tenderness may be found—in a flower in a crannied wall, or in the morning sun on a California beach.[30]

Keen sees three levels of life: the body, the world, and the ultimate context, or mystery, which supports the world. The body is most basic, and man is aware of the body, carnally, primarily through the sense of touch. As man is in his body, so he is in the world. But because man's view of his body determines his view of the world, it also determines his view of the ultimate: for as man is in the world, so he is in the ultimate context. The ultimate context is a horizon that is not really known, for what is known is limited to the immediate experience of the body: "An honest theology is necessarily agnostic." [31] But man has a relation with the ultimate context and, as we have seen, it is primarily dependent on the orientation gained from the body. If one trusts in his body and in his physical negotiations with the world, he can trust in that mystery which is the ultimate context of human life. While man has no knowledge of God, he can be in contact with the sacred, for the sacred is encountered through bodily experience. For Keen, the dance functions as the symbol for the carnal approach to the body, the world, and the sacred.

It should be pointed out that Keen's books are exploratory. He has taken us to lands that are not well charted and shown us beasts that are not kept in our zoos. He has asked us to discern them with wonder and feel them in a dance. But he did not get around to giving us a geology of the land, an ecology of the life, or a diplomacy for the relations between this new world and the old country.

Again, we would ask, Why and how is God—whatever his name might be—interested in promoting wonder and dance? How is man such that wonder and dance can occur, and how are they vital to his well being? And how are the new categories of wonder and dance related to the old notions of truth and goodness or to the traditional view of the experience of the holy?

II

Here, then, is the documentation of what might be a new movement, trend, or fad in contemporary Protestant theology. Who cares? Fads are not that important. What might be more important is that here there are foreshadowed theological notions that could help people to survive and to see more clearly. But are the authors' notions similar in such a way that they foreshadow a single, coherent theological perspective? Is that perspective new? And does that perspective leave unexamined, problems in need of examination?

Prior to our analysis of the books, we said that we would take something on faith. That was that Conrad

Hyers was correct (though not explicit) when he affirmed that the books enunciated themes that are interrelated and new. And with that faith we discussed the books as though they belonged together. Now is the time to move beyond faith to make explicit the convergence of the themes and to indicate how they circumscribe an area of theological inquiry that has previously been neglected.

The most elementary indication of a common theme among the several books is that they seem to be protesting against similar tendencies in the contemporary Western world. Each in its distinctive way decries the domination of the belief that man makes his world by his activity, that man should be manipulator. Some aggressive control may be acceptable; but when the urge to control dominates, the times are bad. The manipulative approach of contemporary man is denounced in each author's critique of the spirit of work. Harvey Cox sees the excessive and celebrative spirit of festivity choked out by hard-nosed industrial man. The antithesis of David Miller's notion of games is serious, purposive work. And the antithesis of Robert Neale's notion of play is work—as it deals with the tensions of conflict. For Sam Keen, the *homo admirans* has been vanquished by *homo faber*. The manipulative approach stifles important imaginative capacities of man. The mind "works" in the sense that it is committed to the sterile reiteration of man's previous intellectual manipulations. It becomes traditional rather than imaginative. The problem with the domination of the manipulative approach is that it puts all reliance on the creation of man and prevents man from being receptive to creation that can come to him. Man places himself in a closed universe, circumscribed by the possibilities realizable by his own decision and effort.

On the other hand, the individual who can balance or overcome activistic manipulation by festivity, fantasy, games, play, wonder, or dance is one who is appreciative —appreciative of possibilities that transcend those of his manipulated world.

> Intuition, ecstasy, and awe open us to this larger cosmic circle. Idea, analysis, and conscious decision relate us to the smaller historical one. (Cox) [32]

> The story is about a movement of an idea out of an originally religious unified configuration, proceeding through a period of fragmentation, individuation, and breakdown, and ending with a rediscovery of an original harmony which had never been forgotten or lost in some forms of Eastern religious wisdom. (Miller) [33]

> When the response of fascination rules over awe, the individual fully surrenders his work self and work world and is precipitated into the world of adventure, receiving the fruits of peace, freedom, delight, and illusion. . . . The loss of the old self and old world would be met by the gain of a new self and new world. (Neale) [34]

> As we shall see in a later chapter, the irreconcilable conflict is . . . between the traditional notion that man lives in wonder in a cosmos already partially informed by patterns of meaning and value, and the modern view that man lives in constant anxiety in

a chaos which he alone must shape and make meaningful. (Keen) [35]

The adumbrations from beyond are apprehended with imagination, which is referred to by Cox as fantasy, by Miller as humor, by Neale as illusion, and by Keen as wonder. They evoke a response of celebration, which is referred to by Cox as festivity, by Miller as games, by Neale as play, and by Keen as dance. In short, the problem is that man has become blind to everything except what his activity manipulates; he must become appreciative of what transcends his manipulation, and this appreciation can be characterized as imagination and celebration.

So the authors are united in rejecting an exclusively activistic approach in a circumscribed world; and they are united in advocating an appreciative approach to a world with a meaningful depth. This is a call for a view of man as an aesthetic being. Man becomes what he should be when he is imaginatively and responsively sensitive. He becomes what he should be when he senses with fantasy, humor, illusion, and wonder and when he responds in a spirit of festivity, games, play, and dance. This is an advocacy of essentially aesthetic qualities of man. Here we are using aesthetics to refer not to the etymological and obsolete root, *aisthesis*, which means simply to sense things perceptible to the senses. Nor are we using the word to refer, in the more contemporary way, to a philosophy or theory of taste, which concentrates on criteria for evaluating the fine arts. Rather, we refer to a distinctive mode of existence or experience, characterized by imaginative awareness and an appreciative response to what that awareness gives. This aesthetic mode of existence is, in the five books, a fresh emphasis on a particular interpretation of man, his religious life and his theological understanding.

Typically, aesthetics refers to beauty, but the four authors seldom use the word "beauty." There is a good reason for avoiding the term. It is a term that is amorphous and one that has received innumerable definitions. Nevertheless, most definitions of beauty would comprehend the imaginative and celebrative responses described by the authors.

Each of the authors argues for the paramount importance of a mode of existence, which we have called the aesthetic mode of existence, by claiming that the particular kind of response that he advocates is beneficial, satisfying, or valuable—in, of, and by itself. The activistic and manipulative approach is only of instrumental value. It is valuable because it does something with the past or brings about something in the future. That is what work is. The aesthetic approach to life has intrinsic value; it is valuable in that it yields worth in itself in the present moment. Harvey Cox will say, "Festivity, like play, contemplation, and making love, is an end in itself. It is not instrumental." [36] Sam Keen will say, "Wonder is the foundation of values because a wondering encounter is the basis of a nonutilitarian approach to things and persons." [37] Neale's "work" is the utilitarian attempt to resolve conflict; while his "play" is the non-utilitarian adventurousness resulting from psychic harmony. The position of Miller is more difficult to assess for he does talk of the four, seemingly utilitarian, "functions" of play. However, these functions are not in fact utilitarian. They center on "non-seriousness," "fiction," "change," and "purposelessness." For Miller, the game is for the play itself and not for the results.

It is this aesthetic approach which causes the new theological constructs hinted at by the four authors. God, however he might be described, is what fosters the aesthetic receptiveness that issues in festivity, fantasy, games, play, wonder, and dance. Faith is the state of openness to the aesthetically stimulating. And the religious life is participation in activities that are valuable in themselves.

In these ways, then, the themes of the books seem to be interrelated and pointing in the same direction: toward an aesthetic approach in life, religion, and theology. But do they point in a *new* direction? To find similarity among five books in theology may be as easy as finding dishonesty among thieves. But without originality this collection of books is not particularly significant.

The direction is new because it points to an aesthetically oriented theology. This is not the area of most historical and systematic theology, which is concerned with establishing the truth of certain notions by pointing toward the past. Truth is not primary in an aesthetically oriented theology. This is not the area of most ethical theology, which is concerned with establishing the proper means of attaining certain results in the future. The good is not primary in an aesthetically oriented theology. This is not the area of most discussions of the nature of the

holy, which are concerned with describing the impact of
the "wholly other." There are a variety of reactions to the
holy in the books discussed, but the phenomenology of the
holy is not the primary element in these aesthetically
oriented theologies. Some might argue that theology
with an aesthetic orientation has been going on in un-
dergraduate and graduate courses in "religion and art."
But the religion and art approach usually seeks particular
religious implications in works of art; for example, literature is often used as a source for moral paradigms or
true Christ figures. A thoroughly aesthetic rendering of
theology would affirm an aesthetic mode of existence, an
aesthetic mode of experience, and an aesthetic mode of
expression. It would work for an aesthetic interpretation
of the nature of revelation, faith, sin, grace, etc. And it
would concentrate, not on the truth of God's word, not
on the goodness of God, and not on God as the holy—
but on God as the lure for beauty.[38] That's new.

Do these four authors, then, leave significant problems
unexamined? Our answer, and our reason for pursuing
the present inquiry, is: Yes, at least three crucial questions absolutely integral to any theological position are
barely touched. Perhaps this is understandable, given the
introductory nature of the books. Nevertheless, the
questions are crucial and neglected.

First, claims have been made for the value of festivity,
fantasy, games, play, wonder, and dance that have traditionally been made for truth, goodness, or the apprehension of the holy. Or, as we said above, the books assert
that a certain (aesthetic) quality of experience is of para-

mount value. This comparative assessment was never made explicit, for in these books there is no consideration of the relative values of the aesthetic, the true, the good, or the apprehension of the holy. Nevertheless, to make an explicit assertion that the aesthetic experience is of paramount value, when that is done in an area where comparable assertions about the intrinsic value of other orientations have claimed such value, is to make implicit denials. The problem is that the explicit assertion and the implicit denials are simply posited without explanation or defense. This is to beg the question. The question of axiological priorities, or priorities among kinds of value, is never met and dealt with, and it needs to be.

In fact, the authors are exceedingly vague even in their descriptions of what might be true, good, and holy. And the relation between their aesthetic mode and these other notions is vague. Robert Neale, when defining faith as make-believe, makes the following comments about the relation of faith and truth on a single page:

> In the religious response, the myth is acknowledged as autonomous. . . . To use Eliade's term, the story is "true" simply because it exists. . . . To judge is to stand outside the story in the profane world, and this is precisely what the religious person cannot do. . . . And for the one who fully participates in the story, *nothing else is required.* Questions of truth and falsity remain irrelevant, indeed, even incomprehensible.[39]

David Miller raises crucial ethical questions without exploring the implications:

We might say that the articles of the creed of contemporary meaning go something like this:

Our day:	playday
Our time:	playtime or recess
Our people:	playboys and playmates
Our world:	playground or playroom
Our society:	games [40]

This leads one to recall M. Conrad Hyers' acknowledgment that these books could seem to herald an untimely
revival of *A Child's Garden of Verses* or *Alice in Wonderland*. For some people can measure days and time in
the number of deaths from starvation, malnutrition, and
war that occur per day, per hour, per minute, per second.
Sometimes "our" people are not playing, but are at each
other's throats with frustrations born of race, class, and
political differences. Our world is polluted and our favor-
ite games are war, nuclear war, genocide, and Armaged-
don. So the ethical implications should not go unnoticed
and unexamined. And Sam Keen can raise the question of the relations between the object of wonder and
the holy, acknowledge the similarity of the two, but never
make it quite clear how he has resolved the question of
their differences.[41]

So the reader is left with questions: What is the nature
of the true, the good, and the apprehension of the holy?
How are they not of intrinsic value? How, by comparison, is the aesthetic experience of intrinsic value? How
can the assertion that aesthetic experience is available in
itself be explained and justified? These questions will be
considered in Chapter II, "The Primacy of Beauty."

Second, earlier we quoted the authors in order to indicate that each affirmed that the orientation which he advocated opened the individual to a larger cosmos—larger than the cosmos circumscribed by the products of human manipulation. Unfortunately, this was about the limit of their metaphysical speculation. Certain metaphysical pictures are foreshadowed but never clearly exposed or developed. Certain roles for God and the sacred are enunciated, but the nature of divine reality and action is never spelled out. For example, the reasons why and how God would want to or be able to foster aesthetic experience are never given. And hints of a new epistemology are given. But the reader is never told how the fresh data for imagination or celebration enter human experience. No metaphysical footing for an epistemology is given. And if there is to be a reordering of values, making the aesthetic paramount, what is the nature of reality, man, and knowledge that makes that reordering desirable? If aesthetic apprehension is of paramount importance, how does it contribute to truth and goodness and the experience of the holy, and how do they contribute to the aesthetic, and what is the character of reality that engenders these contributions?

Our authors have proposed a fundamental reorientation. They have argued for this through the citation of psychological, sociological, literary, popular-cultural, anthropological, phenomenological, religious, and autobiographical data. But a fundamental reorientation finally presupposes a metaphysical reorientation, and until this is discussed the reorientation has not been adequately expressed. The fundamental basis for certain notions cannot remain suspended in air. So, regardless of the current disdain for metaphysics, the question must be pursued. There should be some effort to supply a metaphysical foundation for these notions. One possible metaphysical foundation is projected in Chapter III, "A Rationale for Beauty."

Third, the theological implications of this fresh perspective have been dealt with in an apparently random and selective manner by the authors. Each book concluded with a few remarks on a few theological notions. Harvey Cox discussed theological method, Christology, and faith. David Miller discussed myth, theological language, and faith. Robert Neale discussed the sacred, magic, myth, ritual, death, and irreverence. Sam Keen, in *Apology for Wonder*, discussed grace and gratitude, and in *To a Dancing God* he offered some "Notes for a Visceral Theology." The comments were felicitous and helpful. But the theological output is of such a character that the reader feels that he is being asked to marry a new theological being after learning a little about her lineage and after having been shown an isolated hand and foot. At least an overall sketch might help. So, without the presumption of any real comprehensiveness, Chapter IV, "A Theology of Beauty," will attempt to provide some more extensive comments on aesthetically oriented theology.

The conclusion of this chapter should be greeted with a laugh. We have solemnly announced our intention, in one chapter, to resolve the classic problem of the good, the true, and the beautiful—and the holy; in another chapter, to enunciate a metaphysical basis for aesthetics; and in the last chapter, to show how theology can be re-made. We have only to eschew rigor, and the job can be done. We have only to announce bravely that this is not the time for scholastic thoroughness, and hope the reader can forgive our sin. Or we can plead that our objective is not to make a definitive argument, but merely, with cavalier abandon, to show a type of approach to certain problems.

CHAPTER II

THE PRIMACY OF BEAUTY

Five Dialogues on Life's Meaning:

ON IMMORTALITY

> *That whoever believes in him should not perish but have eternal life.* (John 3:16.)

"Why should we walk?" the shoe asked the foot.

"To get to the end," said the foot.

"And when do we get to the end?" asked the shoe.

"After we stop walking," said the foot.

"We get there *after* we stop walking?"

"Yes, after we stop," said the foot.

"You're putting me on," punned the shoe.

ON TRUTH

And you will know the truth and the truth will make you free. (John 8:32.)

"Why should we walk?" the shoe asked the foot.

"To follow the true course," said the foot.

"And what is the shape of the true course?" asked the shoe.

"It's a straight line, defined by an old map," said the foot.

"And we just go on and on?" asked the shoe.

"Yes. On and on," said the foot.

"Oh, my," said the shoe, and it curled up and put the foot to sleep.

ON GOODNESS

Whoever then relaxes one of the least of these commandments and teach men so, shall be called least in the kingdom of heaven. (Matt. 5:19.)

"Why should we walk?" the shoe asked the foot.

"To keep in step," said the foot.

"What step?" asked the shoe.

"The right step, given by the good drill sergeant," said the foot.

"But I am a civilian shoe and presume to be free," said the shoe.

"Get in step," said the foot.

The shoe turned and twisted and said, "I'm splitting. You can march and bleed and work on your own . . . sole."

ON THE HOLY

I lay my hand on my mouth. (Job 40:4.)

"Why should we walk?" the shoe asked the foot.

The foot gave no answer, but curled four toes under and then slowly, with the big toe, pointed upward.

"Why should we walk?" the shoe shouted—thinking the foot might have missed the question.

"We should walk because there is walking, because it is wholly other than standing still, because it is mysterious, because we choose to walk, because one small step is one great stride and that is the greatest conceivable contradiction realized in the moment. . . ."

"Cease!" said the shoe. "If you will return to mute pointing, I will hold my tongue—for you have unlaced me."

ON BEAUTY

_____ (?)

"Why should we walk?" the shoe asked the foot.

"We probably should not even start, given your average shoe's short life," said the foot.

"Not to mention your average foot's long smell," retorted the shoe.

The foot wriggled and drummed its toes and asked, "Would you find it fitting to accompany me on a walk before dark?"

"If it is interesting," answered the shoe.

No matter how they may have struggled, the shoe and the foot are to be faulted. For they failed to come up with a Biblical maxim appropriate to the fifth dialogue. Surely the Bible must include the category of the aesthetic. Surely Jesus must have had some words on the beautiful or the tragic or the comic. Or, the Bible failing, our theological heritage must include explicit and positive assessment of the aesthetic in its exhaustive representation of God, man, nature, and history.

But, at the same time, the shoe and the foot are to be commended, for at least they did take the trouble to comment on the rival definitions of life's meaning—that life's meaning is found in the reward of immortality, in truth, in the good, or in the experience of the holy. This is more than we can say for the efforts of Messrs. Cox, Miller, Neale, and Keen. While they do assess the direct antitheses to their own affirmations, they give barely a glance at the classic alternatives for life's meaning. Most of their listeners justify their existence by their pursuit of heaven or of truth or of goodness or of the experience of the holy. Their listeners have been carefully taught that beauty is at best avocational and at worst frivolous and irresponsible. Certainly, each of our four authors has something new to sell. But one does not stroll through the square simply announcing that now he has the real elixir. Out of courtesy for the old folks at least, one stops to explain why the old medicines should be flushed.

So, in the interest of emending this oversight, we will attempt to assess briefly the classic alternatives, recognizing all the while that our offering is remarkably superficial, providing no more than an indication of a type of a reaction to truth, goodness, and the experience of the holy.

The initial problem is, On what common ground, with what criterion, can the relative merits of all the alternatives be assessed? We have argued that most of the time [1] the four authors maintain that the aesthetic mode of existence should be of paramount importance for the individual. By implication, the pursuit of immortality, truth, goodness, or the experience of the holy would not be of paramount importance. But, in terms of what criterion, relevant to all alternatives, can claims for paramount importance be fairly assessed? Without such a criterion the claims for the primacy of beauty, or of the rewards of immortality, or of truth, or of goodness, or of the experience of the holy simply stand side by side, unevaluated and unreconciled.

Without great fanfare, we would suggest as a criterion the notion of intrinsic value. Intrinsic value can be defined in terms of the use of experience. Now, right off, this might seem to be a queer move, for use seems naturally to refer to future utility and to the logical opposite of intrinsic value, which is extrinsic value or instrumental value. Though it might be queer, it might also be convenient. For if from the common and utilitarian meaning of use we can wrench away a meaning of use correlative to intrinsic value, we will have a common term for relating intrinsic value and instrumental value. Instrumental value refers to the use of some present event or experience as a means for some future end. An instrumentally valuable use is valuable because of the future condition it brings about. Intrinsic value refers to some present event or experience which is, itself, useful simply for being experienced now. An intrinsically valuable use is valuable because of the present condition that it is. An instrumentally valuable use is useful for something else; an intrinsically valuable use is useful in itself.

Now a pernicious interlocutor might well ask, What kind of condition should use bring about or consist of, if use is to be useful? Of course, future conditions, sought by instrumental uses, can be as various as are the intentions of the individual who is acting instrumentally. But at least it can be said that that condition must be something that is desirable, since it is sought. If it is desirable, it must be satisfying to someone or something. Similarly, the present conditions, which are intrinsic uses, must be useful in themselves because they render some kind of present satisfaction. Use is functioning properly when it brings, or is, satisfaction.

We will argue, then, that the candidacy of a claim for paramount importance can be assessed in terms of the question, Does what you claim is of paramount importance contain intrinsic value? Of course, what in any given moment is of paramount importance might not be intrinsically valuable, or, conversely, what is intrinsically valuable might not be—in that moment—of paramount importance. You might claim that knowing the truth is of paramount importance in life, and that it is intrinsically valuable. But if you fall into a cold well at sunset, it is of paramount importance that you climb out before dark, even though well-climbing may not be intrinsically valuable; conversely, knowing the truth about aquatic life at the bottom of a well may be the kind of thing that is intrinsically valuable, but it is not at that moment of paramount importance. But we are discussing a claim for what is of paramount importance in the meaning of life as a whole, and arguing that that claim can be assessed by the test of intrinsic value.

What is of paramount importance must at some time provide intrinsic value. If it provides only instrumental value, it will never provide the present satisfaction that makes life worth living. With instrumental value alone the present would be meaningful and valuable only to the degree that it would have future consequences. Life would be directed toward the future but never toward the present as itself useful. There would never be experience useful simply for being experienced now. We would continually salivate for the future and never be fed in the present. It is easy to see that most of the time the present works for the future. But if that happened all of the time, life would become as absurd as a circle of men, each conscientiously scratching the back in front of him but never appreciating the back scratching he was getting.

Admittedly, this is complex. Yes, most of life must be spent scratching the other fellow's back. And there might be some immediate satisfaction in scratching backs. But, whatever the source—being scratched or scratching—there must be some moments that themselves are satisfying. There must be something which causes you to say: "O.K., I liked that. I can sweat all day if I can have that. I can die tonight and be able to say that there were a few precious times." If there were not such times why bother to start walking? Why get out of bed? Why ask the race to persist? What loss would there be in extinction? The quality of intrinsic value is what, in the last analysis, makes life worth living.

If the claims for paramount importance can be adjudicated in terms of intrinsic value, how is intrinsic value related to religious faith? Most simply, it is related by identity: The experience of religious faith is intrinsically valuable. Consequently, that experience which is of paramount importance will be a religious faith. But religion refers to God as well as to faith; it concerns objective meanings as well as subjective meanings. With reference to subjective meanings, or faith, religion attempts to deal with a kind of experience that makes life worth living. Religion asks: What is the nature of your ultimate concern? [2] What is the character of your absolute dependence? [3] How do you align your heart and place your trust? [4] That kind of experience which makes life worth living is ultimate or absolute by comparison to other concerns or dependencies in life. That kind of experience gives the ground of meaning to other aspects of life. It does not derive its basic value from something else in the past, nor from something to which it contributes—instrumentally—in the future. If it did derive its basic value from something else, to the extent that it did, that thing would itself be ultimate or absolute. Thus, faith experience is worthwhile in itself. It has intrinsic value. It is useful simply for being experienced now. With reference to objective meaning, religion says that faith experience has intrinsic value when it relates to that objective reality which makes intrinsic value possible. Commonly, that reality is called God. Theologically, God is referred to as that ultimate about which man should be ultimately concerned, or that absolute on which man should be absolutely dependent, or that trustworthy reality in which man should have trust.

Now our objective is to attempt to assess the claims to paramount importance, as they are projected by the classic rivals: the true, the good, the experience of the holy, and the beautiful. The criterion for the assessment will concern intrinsic value: Which of the rivals gives to its advocate intrinsically valuable experience? The consequence of the assessment will be to determine which of the rivals gives to religion an appropriate orientation. For religion purports to espouse that meaning of life which is of paramount importance and which gives intrinsically valuable experience. The assessment will relate primarily to the subjective meaning of religion—the quality of experience appropriate to religion—and only secondarily, and by implication, to the objective meaning of religion—the nature of religion's God.

However, before we proceed with this examination, it should be explained why we will not treat a striving for immortality as a possible aim for life, as it was considered in the dialogues above. As the shoe told the foot, at the outset of our discussion and theirs, seemingly serious entertainment of a future immortality strikes the contemporary listener as a "put-on." No matter at what length one wants to argue that some kind of afterlife is not theoretically impossible, and that it therefore should be a possibility held for further questioning, there is simply not sufficient empirical evidence for the existence of an afterlife to warrant its acceptance. In fact, we all know that almost all the world would be astonished if any empirical evidence—whether direct, indirect, or in terms of effects—for the existence of some kind of afterlife were produced. Yes, the loss of a belief in heaven can be shattering for the youthful. Yes, it still sounds very much better than death. No, it has not been disproven; but then again, neither has astrology or demonology. It is a tenuous subject, indeed, for serious pursuit. And it seems to many to be a foolish and self-serving aim for life.

But with this acknowledgment comes the fear that this life may be all we have. So religion demands that in the interim between birth and death there be some experience useful in itself, some felt satisfaction in present experience.

I. THE TRUE

Truth has many definitions. But whether defined according to the coherence theory or the correspondence theory, whether viewed relativistically or absolutistically, contextually or ideally, whether reached empirically or rationally, whether evaluated pragmatically for its use or romantically for its purity or existentially for its authenticity or symbolically for its connotation or linguistically for its function, truth tells what the case—in any of the various senses—is. But are not all theories of truth correspondence theories of truth? To have the truth is to have within your present mentality some representation that in some way corresponds accurately with a condition outside your present mentality. That which is to be represented can be, according to the various definitions of truth, anything from an action, to a physical object, to a subjective feeling. For each theory of truth stipulates what the nature of reality is; it refers to particular real facts congruent with that nature of reality; and it proceeds to designate as truths, accurate re-presentations to mentality of those real facts.

Even coherence theories of truth in the last analysis are correspondence theories of truth. Coherence theories of truth say that a notion is true, not because it corresponds to some external reality, but because it coheres internally within a scheme of ideas. So notion "C" would be true, not because it corresponds with a given reality, but because it coheres with and amplifies the significance of notions "A," "B," "D," etc. However, coherence theories are usually metaphysical, in that they strive to present the ideal or the really real situation, which runs deeper than superficial realities. And, finally, this is to say that notion "C" is in fact coherent with other notions because notion "C" *corresponds* to a metaphysical reality that is coherently related to the other metaphysical realities corresponding to notions "A," "B," "D," etc.

If truth, then, commonly refers to an idea that corresponds to whatever the case may be, then truth is sheerly descriptive. Truth can have no more value than does description. Description does have the instrumental value of providing information requisite to relevant action and to relevant satisfaction.

Present actions, uninformed by accurate description, ignorant of the truth, will seldom be relevant to the world. Without truth you might find yourself running the wrong way on a football field. Uninformed actions seldom mesh with the world they enter, because they are conceived apart from a knowledge of that world.

And satisfaction apart from truth about what the case is, is ignorant bliss. It is satisfaction abstracted from the world. In principle such satisfaction could, by some small chance, pertain to the world. But the odds are higher that it would be the satisfaction of sheer illusion. It would be shallow satisfaction, divested of the complexity of the given world. It would be the satisfaction of a paraplegic dreaming of running a four-minute mile. It would have the pathos of an idiot's smile.

While truth has these instrumental values, it does not have intrinsic value. To acknowledge that truth is prerequisite to relevant satisfaction is not to say that truth is itself the satisfaction. One man can accurately, or truthfully, view and understand a city and be bored with it. Another can truthfully view the same city and reel with excitement, paint it, whistle in it. Each has the same basic truths about the city; one acquires little satisfaction from these truths while the other derives from these truths great satisfaction.

Now your classic seeker-after-truth, your stout defender

of truth-for-truth's-sake, might protest, saying that we have really dealt with the effects of truth rather than with truth itself. When we deal with truth itself, then we deal with truth as simply a satisfaction to behold, as a glowing object of contemplation. This, it might be argued, is to see truth as intrinsically valuable. Such an argument is certainly not without pedigree. Especially in academic halls, such claims have rung and echoed for centuries.

However, when one listens carefully, the sound is hollow. Usually, when it is said that the contemplation of truth is intrinsically valuable, what is meant is that the contemplation of *new* and *significant* truths is intrinsically satisfying. The newness and significance are what make the truth exciting, stimulating, intrinsically valuable. But newness and significance are qualifications independent of considerations of truth alone; and considerations of truth alone are indifferent to newness and significance. Truth, it has been said, is the description of what the case is. Whatever the case is must be *given* to the one who tells the truth. The one who describes the truth does not invent new and significant insights. If he does, he is moving beyond his role as a mere describer of the given case. The contribution of new and significant hypotheses, which later might be described as new and significant truths, must be engendered by a process extraneous to the truth-describing process itself.

On the ground of truth alone, the new is not in any sense preferable to the old. A truth is merely a description of what the case is. It is no more true that man crossed the space from earth to moon than it is that Caesar crossed the Rubicon. On the ground of truth alone the significant is in no sense preferable to the insignificant. To move from the old to the new, from the less significant to the more significant, is to evolve. Truth has no interest in evolution; it simply describes the given case. On the ground of truth alone, it is just as true that you brushed your teeth last night as it is that the solar system is decaying. On the ground of truth alone there is no way of indicating which is more significant. On the ground of truth alone there is no incitement for discovering the implications of the decay of the solar system or for playing with the relations between the decay of your teeth and the decay of the solar system.

To affirm the value of truth is to affirm the instrumental usefulness of truths. And this affirmation is indifferent to considerations of immediate satisfaction, of newness, and of significance. Of course, speaking descriptively, there are people who will hear all this and still profess for themselves the intrinsic satisfaction of holding even old, insignificant truths. What can be said, but that they are more like curators than inventors, more like antiquarians than adventurers, more like dictionaries than laboratories?

Now this has some bearing on Christian theology, because that theology includes a persisting enlightenment motif. Where that motif is emphasized, Christ is the Savior because he brings a higher truth, a new world, the willing acceptance of which can make for salvation. Here, theology is dogmatics; the Bible is a repository of revelation; and a church is a purveyor of proper confessions received from authoritative spokesmen of the past. The motif is found in a spectrum of traditions ranging from the neo-orthodox position (which argues that Christian affirmation, while not purely intellectual, does clearly presuppose the initial acknowledgment of certain enduring truths) to the fundamentalist position (which argues that Christian existence is set and sustained by the repeated affirmation of a certain minimum set of doctrines). This motif in Christian thought is anchored to one conviction: that to be Christian is first of all to accept within your present mentality a fact or doctrine concerning the significance of Jesus. It is to have the truth: a correspondence between a representation of one's present mentality and certain past facts or dogmas.

And from this essential core the rest follows. Human sin is an epistemological problem, a willing or unwilling ignorance, an orientation to distractions of the flesh rather than to the reality given by God. Salvation is initiated by the new word of the revealer, and is received by one who has faith, which in this case means the present acceptance of the word. From this, and secondary to this, follow conditions such as a new life, freedom, justification, and sanctification. This is a story of enlightenment. And the task of the church is to foster enlightenment by spreading the truth, the good news.

Despite the added coloration and footnotes, this is essentially the message of the Letter to the Romans, which pivots on the assertion: "But now the righteousness of God has been manifested apart from law, although the law and the prophets bear witness to it, the righteousness of God through faith in Jesus Christ for all who believe." (Rom. 3:21–22.) The point is that if one is to partake of the righteousness of God, he must first acknowledge (see Rom. 1:28) and believe that righteousness. "So faith comes from what is heard, and what is heard comes by the preaching of Christ." (Rom. 10:17.) Without truth about the new righteousness of God, salvation by that righteousness is impossible.

Roughly the same goes for the Gospel of John. For, in spite of the special character of spiritual knowing in John, the message boils down to one distinction:

> He who believes in him is not condemned; he who does not believe is condemned already, because he has not believed in the name of the only Son of God. And this is the judgment, that the light has come into the world, and men loved darkness rather than light, because their deeds were evil.[5]

This orientation toward truth is implicit in a positivism of revelation found in most neo-orthodox Protestant theologies of the twentieth century. Here the primary function of Christianity is to impart the truth. Holding particular and static truths provides meaning for life. Questions about the believer's immediate satisfaction or the consequences for his future actions are secondary. And strict adherence to the truth of the given events and dogmas discourages the evolution of Christian doctrine and the examination of the significance of doctrine; for new ideas and evaluations of significance involve considerations beyond considerations of truth.

Friedrich Schleiermacher entertained the hypothesis

that Christian piety might consist in knowing, but he concluded negatively, saying:

> But if piety *is* that knowledge, then the amount of such knowledge in a man must be the measure of his piety. . . . Accordingly, on the hypothesis in question, the most perfect master of Christian Dogmatics would always be likewise the most pious Christian. And no one will admit this to be the case. . . ." [6]

Earlier we argued that truth is not intrinsically valuable. Then we looked at the special Christian claim that the holding of certain Christian truths is intrinsically valuable. But Christian truth seems to provide intrinsic value no more than does any other kind of truth. Those who contend that holding Christian truths offers intrinsic value to life view the earth as a staid theological academy. Until the end of time the purpose of man is to reiterate the Christian "truths." Surely, if the race accepts this, it will gladly die of tedium.

II. THE GOOD

The claim that the pursuit of the good, the moral, the ethical, is that action in common experience which is valuable, or useful, in itself, is now a popular claim. There is a large portion of a whole United States generation—born during or after World War II, educated in or after the 1960's, disabused of the religions of the church and of the state, schooled by crises of domestic and international injustice—who can say, Only ethics remains. Truth is a pawn to power; the holy is trapped in stylized ecclesiastical or cultural forms; and beauty is an unexamined notion used, at best, as a slogan. During this century, in other generations, there have been similar groups. One reason these groups were smaller is that in their time there was not such a persuasive education in the discrepancy between public utterance and actual event as has been recently provided. The group in the most recent generation designates itself as "committed," "concerned," or ethically "outraged." And it is satisfied to devote itself to moral reform. That is enough. Anything else would be self-indulgent or utopian.

Ask such people what action they know to be valuable and they will be sure that acts that eliminate injustice, poverty, war, and needless, premature death are valuable. They will scorn their ancestor moralists: they express disdain for any suggestion that smoking, drinking, dancing, divorce, or card playing involve serious moral questions. Similarly trivial are the modern sins of marijuana, extramarital sex, pornography, and the violation of the law. Concerns about such questions lack weight; they are so *passé* they are embarrassing. When, out of solicitude, this modern moralist does address such questions, he will demonstrate their minor status. They spring from culturally relative norms, they are fed by psychological compensations, and they are marketed for economic purposes. Finally, he will claim that they are as nothing compared to injustice, poverty, war, and needless, premature death; a moral response to these ills requires no explanation or justification.

This is a minimalist ethic. It acknowledges a shortage of answers, and knows nothing of the resplendent answers of traditional maximal ethics. It acknowledges an inability to expound a philosophical or theological base for ethics. It admits no longer having a blueprint for the future. It recognizes the relativity and the conditioned-ness of most ethical norms. But it does hold to a few minimal norms, and treats them as universal. These are the elementary beliefs that at least no one should be treated unjustly or be left to suffer and die from want of basic means of sustenance, and no one should be subjected to the horror of war.

However, if you interrogate someone who holds that such a minimalist ethic describes the intrinsic value in life, he backs on and on, over the horizon. You might begin by asking, "Why should someone be granted a life free of war, injustice, poverty, or premature death?" Such a question is received with either consternation or indignation: "Why? Isn't it obvious that people have a right to such freedom!" But the question can be pressed: "Well, what in such a free life makes it valuable?" But again, such a query is greeted with bewilderment. So the questioning must be continued: "Is a life free of injustice, poverty, war, and needless, premature death simply good in itself? Is that good enough for you?" The new moralist might respond: "Hell, no. If you care, you cannot luxuriate in mere freedom from pain. So long as anyone still suffers, no one should rest. So, in turn, I would expect the human I have freed from pain to go out and free others from pain." If you like to speculate, you might then ask, "What do you do when human suffering is conquered?" The moralist might say, "That time will never come," or, "I will deal with that when the time comes."

Now this seems problematic because the new moralist seems to be able to affirm no objective for moral action except the reiteration of that action itself. There is no moment for appreciation of intrinsic value, but only a call for new instrumental action at the moment when old instrumental objectives are accomplished. But is that all there is? Are we being asked simply to go on, never asking for a moment satisfying in itself or a quality of satisfaction that might make the procedure as a whole worthwhile? Do we consume life simply supporting life, never attaining that point when a moment in life is itself valuable or when life in its totality is itself appreciated?

We have attempted to criticize this "minimalist ethic" as, finally, incapable of providing for intrinsic value in life. It fails because it does not provide for a *realization* of satisfaction; and an orientation in life that fails to provide for a realization of satisfaction fails to provide an intrinsic value for life. It can be argued that any particular ethical approach, when examined with regard to its ability to provide intrinsic value in life, suffers from the same basic defect. We cannot exhaustively defend such a generalization here. But we can outline the basic reasons for the generalization through a discussion of the two types of philosophical ethics usually deemed the most elementary by the average textbook: teleological and deontological ethics.

Ethics is the analysis of certain ways of acting, and moral activity is activity in accord with these ways of acting. For teleological ethics these ways of acting are means for attaining desired ends. Teleological ethics in the broadest sense, a sense including utilitarian, situational, and pragmatic ethics, is ethics that says that the means become ethically and morally worthy to the extent that they result in bringing about certain desired ends—such as happiness. While the ends striven for may eventually be of intrinsic value, these ends are not, for the teleologist, moral entities. So, if there is to be intrinsic value in ethics for the teleological ethicist, it must be found in the active means for attaining the ends.

But do these means ever provide the satisfaction appropriate to intrinsic value? The teleologist, in a particular instance, might reason thus: action that brings about the giving of food to a starving child is ethical action; it is a means to a certain desired end. However, the end—the consumption of food by the starving child—is not an ethical act. The consumption of the food by the starving child might be to that child intrinsically satisfying, but to the teleologist that is not an ethical act. To the teleologist that child might with a full stomach be enabled to act effectively to pursue desired ends. So the consumption of the food might have ethical consequences and then become an ethical means of acting. However, when so viewed, the consumption of the food is no longer viewed *as* intrinsically valuable. Rather, it is extrinsically, or instrumentally, valuable as a means to other ends. And those ends, when realized, become means for new ends.

An infinite regress of means sets in. The appreciation of ends, valuable for being presently experienced, is infinitely postponed. Satisfaction is aimed at but never realized in the present. This is the same problem as that encountered in the "minimalist ethic." Teleological action fails to provide intrinsic satisfaction, or experience useful simply for being experienced now.

Deontological ethics would seem to be able to avoid this kind of criticism, for deontological ethics will argue that the means, when dominated by good will, are the sole good, regardless of consequences. Immanuel Kant, defending the intrinsic value of a good will and, by implication, activity guided by a good will, says:

> Even if it should happen that, owing to special disfavor of fortune, or the niggardly provision of a stepmotherly nature, this will should wholly lack power to accomplish its purpose, if with its greatest efforts it should yet achieve nothing, and there should remain only the good will . . . then, like a jewel, it would still shine by its one light, as a thing which has whole its value in itself.[7]

If the present action, when prompted by a good will, is itself intrinsically valuable, an infinite postponement of intrinsic value can be avoided. Look simply to the immediate ethical action itself, and the intrinsic value for life is there. For example, to cite Kant's first categorical imperative, if you act in a way such that you could will that your mode of conduct at that moment should be a universal law, you are acting ethically in that moment, and that is intrinsically valuable.

But what is the satisfaction implicit in such conduct? On the explicit level Kant maintains that motivations involving a desire for the satisfaction of doing the good are antithetical to proper ethical motivation; the actions caused by such motivations have no moral worth. "For the maxim lacks the moral import, namely that such actions be done *from duty*, not from inclination." [8] But can an aim in life give intrinsic value if it spurns considerations of present satisfaction?

On a less explicit level Kant seems to acknowledge that the ethical aim must include consideration of future satisfaction. First, one basis for Kant's first categorical imperative is that it banks, in an instrumental way, against unpleasant consequences. If you act so that you could will that your mode of conduct should be universal law, you will avoid certain unpleasant consequences in the future. For example, when arguing against the ethical legitimacy, in certain exceptional cases, of making a lying promise, Kant notes that such lies issue in two unfortunate results:

> Then I presently become aware that while I can will the lie, I can by no means will that lying should be a universal law. For with such a law there would be no promise at all, since it would be in vain to allege my intention in regard to my future action to those who would not believe this allegation, or if they over-hastily did so would pay me back in my own coin.[9]

In other words, if you lie, you will suffer from a reputation of untrustworthiness or from being lied to yourself. Kant will argue that a prudential motive for truth-telling, a motive directed toward consequences free of such problems, is not a valid ethical motive. One should be truthful from the motive of duty alone. Nevertheless, Kant is interested in making it clear that dissatisfaction does accrue for one who acts unethically. John Stuart Mill also argues that Kant is concerned with future satisfaction, or desirable consequences:

> But when he [Kant] begins to deduce from this precept [the first categorical imperative] any of the actual duties of morality, he fails, almost grotesquely, to show that there would be any contradiction, any logical (not to say physical) impossibility, in the adoption by all rational beings of the most outrageously immoral rules of conduct. All he shows is that the *consequences* of their universal adoption would be such as no one would choose to incur.[10]

Second, Kant seems to implicitly acknowledge that the ethical aim involves satisfaction, as he argues that there must be immortal life and that that life must allow for the happiness proportionate to the morality of the individual. Again, Kant argues that ethical motivation concerns devotion to duty alone and never concerns the attainment of the happiness of immortal life. Nevertheless, Kant insists that in a moral universe morality must eventually issue in the satisfaction or happiness of heaven.[11]

The question arises: When satisfaction is seen to be an implicit justification for ethical action, does an implicit teleological ethic become apparent, where there is a concern with the instrumental means of acquiring a future satisfaction? If this happens, then Kant's ethic on an implicit level would be just as implicated in the continual postponing of satisfaction as would an avowedly teleological ethic. For example, you would not lie today so that you can contribute to trustworthiness tomorrow. Tomorrow you will be concerned, not with the satisfaction of trustworthy relations, but with honesty, so that trustworthiness will prevail the next day. Hence, satisfaction would not be appreciated in the present moment.

Then two comments about deontological ethics as represented by Kant are possible. Explicitly, satisfaction has no place; so if there is to be intrinsic value in this ethical orientation, it is not intrinsic value as we have defined it, because it is without satisfaction. Implicitly, satisfaction has a place, but in the future; here the ethic appears to be instrumental, postponing the realization of the satisfaction, or intrinsic value, aimed at. It could be argued that this implicit ethic is Kant's most basic ethic, for it is this ethic that becomes apparent when Kant elaborates his own position.

The conclusion, therefore, seems to be that neither teleological nor deontological ethics can involve real intrinsic value, since teleological ethics postpones the realization of intrinsic value, and deontological ethics either does the same thing or proposes a present value, but a value without satisfaction. If it were accepted that Kant's most basic ethic is his implicit ethic, there would be limited evidence—including "minimalist ethics," teleological ethics, and one interpretation of deontological ethics— for a radical simplification: all ethics is properly concerned with means and instrumental value alone. Intrinsic value would not properly pertain to ethics. Intrinsic value is aimed at but never felt in ethical activity.

This is hardly an original objection. There is evidence that certain authors of the Old Testament also were disturbed that ethical obedience to Yahweh did not include intrinsic value or satisfaction. So they became interested in the problem of how ethical action could eventuate, teleologically, in future satisfaction. The members of the Deuteronomic school argue valiantly for the retributive philosophy of history—the theory that there is a strict correlation between obedience to Yahweh and historical destiny. When Israel is obedient to Yahweh, it will prosper; when it is disobedient, it will fail. While concern about future prosperity or failure was not meant to be the motivation for obedience to Yahweh, apparently it was felt that obedience should be at least associated with satisfaction. However, even a belief in this association was rejected by the authors of Job and Ecclesiastes. Job, a good man suffering misfortune, felt constrained to say:

Why are not times of judgment kept by the Almighty, and why do those who know him never see his days? (Job 24:1.)

And Ecclesiastes either saw no correlation between ethical merit and satisfaction or toyed with the possibility that there was a perverse correlation:

Again I saw that under the sun the race is not to the swift, nor the battle to the strong, nor bread to the wise, nor riches to the intelligent, nor favor to the men of skill; but time and chance happen to them all. (Eccl. 9:11.)

> In my vain life I have seen everything; there is a
> righteous man who perished in his righteousness,
> and there is a wicked man who prolongs his life in
> his evil-doing. (Eccl. 7:15.)

Now it can be argued that this absence of correlation between ethical obedience and satisfaction contributes to
the Hebrews' late emphasis on a satisfaction beyond
history—through apocalypticism or in a hope for immortality. But leaving such hypotheses aside, it does seem
that the Hebrews were concerned about the absence of
satisfaction in the ethical way of life.

Have we been high-handed? Have we been cavalier with
those who might argue that the ethical orientation in life
is intrinsically valuable? If our critique is valid, why have
people oriented toward ethics adopted this position?

In the spirit of contemporary philosophy, we might cope
with the last question by an analysis of language. There
seems to be a semantic confusion that might prompt
people to think of moral activity as intrinsically satisfying. The word "good" is used in two important ways.
Plato faced this. He noted that there were things good-
in-themselves and things good because they brought
things good-in-themselves.

> Are there not some [goods] which we welcome for
> their own sakes, and independently of their conse-
> quences, as, for example, harmless pleasure and
> enjoyments, which delight us at the time, although
> nothing follows from them.[12]

> And would you not recognize [a class of goods]
> such as gymnastic, and the care of the sick, and

the physician's art; also the various ways of money-making—these do us good but we regard them as disagreeable; and no one would choose them for their own sakes, but only for the sake of some reward or result which flows from them? [13]

These definitions have been enshrined in two designations: intrinsic goods and instrumental goods. However, the two meanings often are melded so that the word "good" is used to refer to both meanings simultaneously. Specifically, it often occurs that the intrinsic value appropriate to intrinsic good is assigned to the instrumentally good actions, so that they are viewed as intrinsically valuable.

This confusion is analogous to the confusion of one who sets out to acquire the instrumentality of money so that he can have the satisfactions that money buys, but who becomes so conditioned to the association between the holding of money and the benefits that money buys that he comes to value money itself. He begins to hoard and fondle money. Studies have indicated that financial wizards are more interested in making money than in the uses of money.

This mistake is relevant to the confusion in ethics. We have argued that ethics concerns actions that are not intrinsically valuable, because they do not allow for the present realization of value or satisfaction. Hence, all ethics—except possibly deontological ethics on the explicit level—in the last analysis directly concern only instrumental means. Nevertheless, people consider ethical action to be intrinsically valuable. Now we would argue that this error might occur because people have become so accustomed to the association between the instrumental means and the intrinsically valuable ends that they are to cause, that they begin to think of the instrumental means as intrinsically valuable. They have melded the definitions so that the intrinsic value appropriate to the intrinsically valuable end is thought to inhere in the instrumental means.

So we hear sacrifice praised as valuable in itself, despite the fact that sacrifice is a purely instrumental means for attaining an intrinsic good beyond the sacrifice. Or we hear justice praised as intrinsically valuable, despite the fact that justice is only a social means that creates a context for individual satisfactions. And the same could be said for those who advocate as the intrinsic value in life, the work of eliminating war, poverty, and needless, premature death: they have transferred the intrinsic value that is appropriate to the goals of ethical action, to its means, and have come to think that simply acting ethically is intrinsically valuable.

In life-style, the logical extreme of this confusion is masochism—where the desired ends are forgotten and the painful means for reaching these ends become the sole preoccupation. You find people proud of exhaustion and its signs—such as bags under the eyes, pale faces, ulcers, and even nervous breakdowns. A stock compliment is for a wife to tell her husband he is overworked. Politicians, especially campaigning politicians, often put out, as part of an image enhancement, stories about the long hours they work and the few hours they sleep.

(Henry Cabot Lodge in 1960 and Eugene McCarthy in 1968 were automatically censured because they got enough sleep while campaigning.)

Christian ethics concentrates on means also. Christian moral action functions as the means for the actualization of the will of God. Traditionally, these means of ethical action are not meant to be paramount; the good is not done because doing the good action is itself the paramount and intrinsic value. For example, love is valued, not in itself as an intrinsic value, but only as an instrumental means for fulfilling the will of God. Listen to Rudolf Bultmann discussing Jesus' ethic in *Jesus and the Word:*

> These are emphatic passages, but they are so few that it is plain to be seen that neither Jesus nor his church thought of establishing by this demand for love a particular program of ethics. Rather the demand for love is included under the general requirement of doing the will of God.[14]

> He knows nothing of *doing good for good's sake*; the idea that every good deed is its own reward is foreign to him.[15]

Or Emil Brunner in *The Divine Imperative:*

> There is no such thing as an "intrinsic Good." . . . It [God] is he who unites what is with what ought to be, He, the Creator of nature and of the spirit, of all that exists and of ideas; His will is the source of that which is and ought to be.[16]

In short: traditionally, the Christian ethical orientation receives its ends or goals from God, and its means of ethical action are only of instrumental value.

What then of those who, as Christians, say the ethical orientation is paramount? There are signs that such a position was implicit in the language of some churchmen in the 1960's. It is said that the Christian's place is in the street rather than the sanctuary, beside his brother rather than with his Bible, and that his message is simply: love. Emphasis on political neutrality, ecumenicism, liturgical reform, and questions of church organization should move to the rear where they belong. Room should be made for a concern for one's fellowman to shoulder in at the front. It is not the dogmatician's passion for true doctrine, not the existentialist's or mystic's voluptuous psychic quivers, but, after all, the need or obligation to love one's neighbor that should dominate the Christian perspective.

This ethic is Christian because it claims that the will of the Biblical God is the only sufficient cause for moral action. God's commands require obedience. But it also claims that the meaning of life is obedience to God. It is this second affirmation that is crucial for ethics. To acknowledge that the will of God is what prompts your ethical action is to describe the end for your ethical actions. That end—the fulfilled will of God—is not an ethical condition, any more than the full belly of a starving child is an ethical condition. But to say that the meaning of my life is that I am one who is obedient to God is to say that the intrinsic value of my life is to *be* a *means* for the end, which is the fulfillment of the will of God. Here Christian moral action is claimed to be intrinsically valuable.

What can be made of this latter claim? First, we are confronted with the anomaly discussed earlier: a means is not intrinsically satisfying, yet it is claimed to be intrinsically valuable. But Christians have a ready answer for this: of course the Christian way is hard and sacrificial, but this is as it should be. This is Christian asceticism. The Christian way of life is a way of suffering. Usually this asceticism is not sincere. Usually it is fraudulent sacrifice secretly motivated by the hopes for hedonism in heaven. It is a prudential, egoistic hedonism: sacrifice today and have the reward of dancing girls after you die; love your neighbor so as to use your neighbor as a means for earning selfish rewards. But, if one is sincere, he tries simply to become a means for fulfilling the will of God; this is the meaning of life. This is an example of the common phenomenon of reveling in obedience, of enjoying slavery. This is to deny human dignity because it advocates a way of life devoid of human satisfaction. This is to be an "Uncle Tom" for God. This is to propose that man become an automaton for a world boss, that man march to the beat of the divine will without missing a step—and like it.

In summary, when it is asserted that the ethical orientation is of paramount importance, two problems seem to arise. First, the appreciation of intrinsic value is continually postponed. Second, with regard to Christian ethics, man becomes subservient; he is so dedicated to the eventual fulfilling of the will of God that present satisfaction and intrinsic value are obviated.

III. THE HOLY

We have argued that neither an orientation toward the true nor an orientation toward the good can be intrinsically valuable. But there are those who would argue that, of course, the predominant orientation for theology and religion should be neither epistemological nor ethical. To adopt one of these orientations would be to substitute a human value—truth or goodness—for the holiness of God. This argument is the entree for those who would argue that theology should be oriented toward the holy. Let God be God! God is Wholly Other! God and the world are discontinuous and any effort to see intrinsic value in terms of truth or goodness presumes that God and the world are continuous. The same strictures, it should be noted, are leveled against the notion that aesthetic experience is intrinsically valuable. Jaroslav Pelikan, in *Fools for Christ*,[17] defends the primacy of the holy against all the major rivals. He attempts to show that those who have made truth, goodness, or beauty intrinsically valuable in their religious lives have domesticated God. We should affirm, Pelikan says, that the holy, while perhaps present in truth, goodness, and beauty, stands above them and is alone the proper object of our religious attention.

From Pelikan's book we learn little about what the holy means or how it is relevant to present experience. But perhaps this is to be expected of those who argue that the paramount orientation in religion and theology should be toward the holy. They say that what is alone of intrinsic value is an ineffable relation with the ineffable holy. But what is the function of such a claim? It seems to work as a negation. It seeks to deny that any human specifications can delineate God, and it argues that characterizations of God in terms of truth, goodness, or beauty impose human specifications on God. Now, if such a denial is consistent, it will not then proceed to provide, in the place of the rejected human specifications, new human specifications. In short, the *via negativa* is pursued. Man is denied conceptual approaches to God; he is left standing before a holy void. So why fault Pelikan for his failure to go on to tell the reader what he means by the holy or how it is relevant to present experience? Perhaps to do so would be inconsistent.

But can this orientation toward the holy be of intrinsic value? To state it negatively, how can an experience (of the holy) that is conceptually vacuous function to provide the paramount orientation, the intrinsic value for an individual's life? It is conceivable that a noncognizable experience can provide a measure of meaning for man. But man is to a degree a cognitive creature. Can a noncognizable experience orient man's ultimate concern or his absolute dependence? Or can it be useful simply for being experienced? Can a noncognizable orientation provide intrinsic value for a cognizing being? I have had the mysteries of the holy commended to me, but I have been left only mystified. Often, when long distance calls are received at home, we say to my little daughter, "Quiet! It's long distance!" She is—sometimes—adequately intimidated and almost always puzzled.

The rejection of the experience of the holy, on the grounds that it is noncognizable, would come as no surprise to those advocating a relation with the holy. This can be illustrated by reference to two famous expositions about the experience of the holy. Rudolf Otto, in *The Idea of the Holy*, interrupts his discourse on the holy for a gentle aside to the reader:

> The reader is invited to direct his mind to a moment of deeply-felt religious experience, as little as possible qualified by other forms of consciousness. Whoever cannot do this, whoever knows no such moments in his experience, is requested to read no farther; for it is not easy to discuss questions of religious psychology with one who can recollect the emotions of his adolescence, the discomforts of indigestion or, say, social feelings but cannot recall any intrinsically religious feelings.[18]

Mircea Eliade, in *The Sacred and the Profane*, says:

> But it is only in the modern societies of the West that nonreligious man has developed fully. Modern nonreligious man assumes a new existentialist situation; he regards himself solely as the subject and agent of history and he refuses all appeal to transcendence. . . . Man *makes himself*, and he only makes himself completely in proportion as he desacralizes himself and the world.[19]

In short, Otto and Eliade are aware that some modern men no longer discern the holy, and the implication is that, obviously, those men are missing out on something of paramount importance and intrinsic value.

It seems that expounders of the holy have pretty well boxed the term in. Otto characterizes the holy in terms of the nonrational responses it induces: the repulsion of the *tremendum* and the attraction of the *fascinans*. The rational attributes of deity are related to the nonrational or suprarational attributes as predicates are related to a subject. "That is to say, we have to predicate them of a subject which they qualify, but which in its deeper essence is not, nor indeed can be, comprehended in them; which rather requires comprehension of quite a different kind." [20] What is distinctive about the holy is that it is ineffable—"in the sense that it completely eludes apprehension in terms of concepts." [21] Eliade introduces *The Sacred and the Profane* by saying that, while Otto concentrated on the irrational aspect of the holy, "we propose to present the phenomenon of the sacred in all its complexity, and not only in so far as it is *irrational*." [22] For a second or two some readers may feel that they are less likely to be defined out. But two sentences later Eliade says, "The first possible definition of the *sacred* is that it is the *opposite of the profane*." [23] The sacred is revealed in a hierophany: "the manifestation of something of a wholly different order, a reality that does not belong in our world, in objects that are an integral part of our natural 'profane' world." [24] If the holy belongs to another world, is not the man who is at home in his world just as estranged from the holy as when it is described as quite irrational?

Those people who are happy to be at home in the world are annoyed when they are officially denied access to the holy. When they are confronted with stark alternatives (the rational and the nonrational, the profane and the sacred), when they are told that the latter is the realm of the holy, when they are told to stop reading if they cannot discern this realm, or when they are referred to as those who would make themselves, they are fenced off from the holy.

In other words, people who orient themselves cognitively like to think that whatever is of intrinsic value is, to a significant degree, cognizable. For them the traditional dichotomies, which place the essence of the holy beyond the rational, or the sacred wholly beyond the profane, do not make sense. For them, if there is to be a glimmering of the divine, it must come as intimately associated with the intelligible and the earthly. The experience of a remote holy is too unintelligible to be intrinsically satisfying.

IV. THE BEAUTIFUL

Now the religious dimension of experience concerns that which is intrinsically valuable, and religion and theology have been traditionally oriented toward the true, the good, and the experience of the holy. We have attempted, very superficially and without any claim to conclusiveness, to indicate ways in which it can be argued that the true, the good, and the experience of the holy do not now concern that which is intrinsically valuable for many people. If such arguments were to be accepted, then there would be need for a new orientation for religion and theology. The value that might provide such orientation must be more than mere truth, in that it must provide for satisfaction in its entertainment, and novelty and significance in its realization. It must be other than purely ethical, in that it must provide for some immediate satisfaction, rather than satisfaction indefinitely postponed, or subservience. And it must offer greater intelligibility than the experience of the holy is said to offer.

Of course, our purpose is to establish that aesthetic experience will overcome these deficits and, consequently, serve as intrinsically valuable experience. Beauty is realized in the subject's own present experience; it is not directed either toward what the objective case before the subject was, toward what the future state beyond the subject will be, or toward a reality that is wholly other than the subject. It is not fixed to the tedium of merely translating the past objective case into present definition —as holds in the search for truth. It is not fixed in subservience or stalled in the treadmill of working for future states that are never appreciated but always sought—as holds in the struggle for the good. It is not distracted by the shock of a reality that is remote—as holds in the experience of the holy. Spatially, beauty is felt as experience *of and in the subject*—rather than as experience of the past *case* of truth, or of the future *state* of the good, or of the remote *reality* of the holy. Temporally, beauty refers to an event *in the present*—rather than to the *past* case of truth, the *future* state of the good, or the *remote* reality of the holy.[25]

Hence, beauty concerns a space and a time which are

actual; and this makes it possible that beauty is, itself, useful simply for being experienced now, and that it is, itself, satisfying. To be felt, satisfaction must have a context; it must be felt in the presence of experience and in experience that is present. Truth, because it is oriented toward an objective case in the past, seems to provide no such context. Goodness, because it is oriented toward a result in the future or a will of God, seems to provide no such context. And the experience of the holy, because it is oriented toward a reality that is remote, seems to provide no such context.

The experience of beauty involves, in addition to the context for satisfaction, the quality of satisfaction. By definition, the experience of beauty is stimulating. To speak of a beauty that is boring is to speak in contradictions. So where there is an experience of beauty, there is, at least, the satisfaction that is found in stimulation. Truth, because it is a reiteration of what the case is, does not necessarily provide the stimulation of novelty or fresh significance. Hence, it can be and usually is productive of the boredom of reiteration. Morality, because it is oriented toward the realization of the future results, or a will of God, usually is unwilling to permit an interest in present benefits. Hence, it can be and usually is productive of the boredom of earnest sacrifice. The quest for the holy, because it is oriented toward that which is quite strange, usually calls for acquiescence to that which is unintelligible. Hence, it can be and often is productive of the boredom of confusion.

The experience of beauty can provide both the context for, and the quality of, satisfaction. And whatever can provide this would seem to provide for religion and theology an orientation toward that which is of intrinsic value. But an aesthetic religious and theological orientation can make sense only if it is supplied with an appropriate philosophical grounding and a distinctive interpretation of the aesthetic character of theology and religion. It is to the task of providing these that we will proceed.

CHAPTER III

A RATIONALE FOR BEAUTY

I

It must be understood that most of the foregoing will make little sense if an important philosophical premise is not accepted. It is regrettable that the disclosure of this premise has been postponed until the third chapter. However, it cannot be denied that it has appeared at the *very beginning* of the third chapter.

This is the premise: An individual is more accurately represented by a bubble in a stream than by a boulder in a desert. He is more adeptly symbolized by lightning in a turbulent sky than by sun in a clear firmament. Heraclitus said:

> You cannot step twice into the same river, for other waters go ever flowing on.[1]

But Parmenides said:

> There remains, then, but one word by which to express the true road: is. And on this road there are many signs that what is has no beginning and never

will be destroyed: it is whole, still, and without end.
It neither was nor will be, it simply is—now altogether, one, continuous! [2]

So Raphael Demos said:

Heraclitus, whom Plato later called the river-philos-
opher, had taught that all things are in flux and that
reality is like a river in which one cannot step twice;
to be is to change. Parmenides maintained the opposite doctrine that to be is to be permanent and
change is an illusion; reality is one, indivisible, and
timeless.[3]

We say:

If you want to nail down a BIG philosophical
point, drive it back to the pre-Socratics.

Heraclitus was closer to the truth than Parmenides. Process—not permanence—is more fundamental to reality.

And in recent philosophy the best philosopher of process is Alfred North Whitehead, who said:

Without doubt, if we are to go back to that ultimate, integral experience, unwarped by the sophisti-
cation of theory, that experience whose elucida-
tion is the final aim of philosophy, the flux of things
is one ultimate generalization around which we
must weave our philosophical system.[4]

Whitehead acknowledges that "there is a rival notion,
antithetical to the former." [5]

Accordingly we find in the first two lines of a famous hymn a full expression of the union of the
two notions in one integral experience:

Abide with me
Fast falls the eventide

Here the first line expresses the permanences,
"abide," "me," and the "Being" addressed; and the
second line sets these permanences amid the in-
escapable flux. Here at length we find formulated
the complete problem of metaphysics.[6]

But, for Whitehead, process and permanence are not
equally basic. Whitehead rejects the notion that things
have a permanent substance or essence, and that they
suffer only superficial change. While he holds for both
process and permanence, Whitehead argues that process
is more basic than permanence and that permanence
only qualifies process.

The influence of process is so fundamental that it in-
fects what seems most clearly to endure: the identity of
individuals. Commonly, we think that oceans may roll,
winds may blow, dust may swirl, forests may spread, and
crowds may disperse; we think of groups as changing.
But, by comparison, it seems that the individuals which
make up those groups are relatively stable. A molecule
of water in an ocean, just as a person within a crowd,
seems to be a permanency within process. Certainly, a person—like other individuals—does not seem to be completely permanent; we think of a person as undergoing
influences. But we continue to think of that person, as
a single person through time, receiving alterations due to
the process that surrounds him. Commonly, we think that
an individual is like a relatively stable raft in a relatively
processive river during a day's float; certainly, the raft

can be worn and nicked and damaged by the processes in the river, but it is the same raft receiving the influences. But Whitehead's metaphysic of process would call for another image. An individual would be more like a ripple of water: it is in process, so that from moment to moment it is a new ripple, and it is affected by the process that surrounds it. Given this predominance of process, an individual does not endure through time; an individual is an event, a puff of experience at a moment of time. Similar individuals, preceding the individual of that moment, and commonly identified with the individual of that moment, are in the past, gone forever. Similar individuals, succeeding the individual of that moment, and commonly identified with the individual of that moment, are in the future, not yet actual. What is commonly thought of as an individual person through time—such as John Smith—is, in fact, a succession of rather similar individual persons, each arising as its moment arrives, and each perishing as its moment passes. Because of the predominance of process, what is actual is a present event. That same event does not endure through time; it is in the moment, and it passes at the termination of that moment. Of course, there can be strong similarities between events, so that the John Smith of this moment is very similar to the event we called John Smith a moment ago. Nevertheless, they are new and different events.

Process predominates. What *is* is a phase of process enacting . . . NOW. Permanence resides not in individuals, but in certain metaphysical conditions that all individuals must always work within. Whitehead says that "the process is itself the actuality. . . ." [7] "Its [an entity's] 'being' is constituted by its 'becoming.' " [8]

To state the matter in a more comprehensive way:

> "Creativity" is the universal of universals characterizing ultimate matter of fact. It is the ultimate principle by which the many, which are the universe disjunctively, become the one actual occasion, which is the universe conjunctively. It lies in the nature of things that the many enter into complex unity.[9]

With this description of the process of creativity, Whitehead places process, or becoming, at the heart of reality, but also amplifies the meaning of process. Process entails relativity. There is not only no unchanging substance in an individual. There is also no isolated substance in an individual, where isolation means that relations with the world may externally influence the individual, but leave his substance unchanged. A process view of reality would affirm that the "many" of the past are the internal constituents of the present "one." So from moment to moment the "one" now becomes a different "one" than the "one" before, because the "many" constituents change from moment to moment. So an individual is simply a present conjunction of many past events—the universe disjunctively—in the present process of making what it will of those events—to become the universe conjunctively. If process eliminates the individual as an unchanging, isolated substance passing from past to present to future, it leaves only the many conjoining into a new one each moment. So John Smith yesterday is a different "one," conjoining a different set of "many's," than John

Smith today, conjoining a new set of "many's." John Smith on Friday might be a man affected by computers, luncheons, cocktails, and business colleagues. John Smith on Saturday might be a man affected by a tramp through the woods, a barbeque, and children. John Smith today is not yesterday's John Smith passed over into today; he is a new conjunction of a new set of relations. So process entails internal relate-ivity, or the notion that the many enter into the one:

> For each relationship enters into the essence of the event: so that, apart from that relationship, the event would not be itself. This is what is meant by the very notion of internal relations.[10]

Earlier we compared an individual to a ripple of water. Here, with relativity in mind, we can expand the metaphor by comparing an individual to the ripple that results from the intersection of earlier ripples.

Now the notion of process and the corollary of relativity are set forth as metaphysical ideas. That is, Whitehead claims that they are generalities relevant to everything that happens. But common sense shuns the full implications of process and relativity. Granted, every schoolboy knows that the apple in his desk, if forgotten and left, will change into a rotten, stinking substance only remotely resembling an apple, and that this process is due to relations affecting the apple, such as the temperature in his desk. (He knows, for example, that a refrigerated desk would retard the decay.) He can even imagine that his desk, if left in the classroom for a million years, would change into a crumbly ash. But at the same time he feels that he himself has an enduring identity; changes may happen to him, but he remains the same boy through such change. So he cannot accept process or relativity as generalities relevant to everything that happens.

We cannot here defend to every schoolboy why the process view of reality applies even to humans. Our task is to defend the primacy of the aesthetic orientation by supporting that orientation with a metaphysical basis. In Chapter I, concentrating on analysis, we suggested that the four authors had provided only a partial and superficial defense of the place and role of the aesthetic. And in Chapter II we argued that the aesthetic is that value which is of paramount importance, because it is intrinsically valuable, while the true, the good, and the experience of the holy are not of paramount importance, because they are not intrinsically valuable. Here, working metaphysically, we will argue that a view of reality as processive will provide an explanation for the paramount importance and intrinsic value of the aesthetic.

II

Near the end of Chapter II we argued that there must be a context for the experience of intrinsic value. This is a minimal prerequisite. Intrinsic value must happen in the space of the subject's own experience and in the time of the present: it must be felt in the presence of experience and in the experience that is present. Once we accept reality as processive, the metaphysical warrant for this claim becomes apparent. If what is actual is in process, and if what is in process exists as a puff of present experience, then intrinsic value must happen in the space and time of present experience. Process has isolated the individual and circumscribed what is, for him, actual. The past has fallen away, the future is not yet. So an individual has only his experience in the present: thus, whatever is intrinsically valuable must be found in one's own experience in the present. Earlier, it was argued that the true, the good, and the experience of the holy refer primarily to spaces other than one's own experience and to times other than the present. But now it can be said that if one claims that there is intrinsic value in the true, the good, or the experience of the holy, then one is presupposing a substance view of reality. For one is talking as though it makes no difference that the referent is a past case (re: the true) or a future state (re: the good) or a remote space (re: certain religious definitions of the good [11] and of the holy). This is to assume that the past, the future, and the remote are in a sense actual and with us, which is to assume that there are substances devoid of process, remaining constant through place and time. One thinks of Parmenides: "It neither was nor will be, it simply is—now, altogether, one, continuous!" [12] A process orientation would not claim that truth, goodness, and the experience of the holy are without value. But it would require that what is of intrinsic value must refer to present experience, because present experience alone is actual. Values which refer primarily to what is not actual could not be intrinsic values. Truth refers to cases that are no more (that occurred outside the subject's experience in the past) and goodness sometimes refers to states that are not yet (that will occur outside the subject's experience in the future) and the holy and religious definitions of the good refer to something remote (strange to the subject's place). By contrast, aesthetic experience refers to and incorporates something that happens in present experience. Aesthetic experience refers to something that originates in actuality, in the present experience of the subject through the acts of imagination, fantasy, illusion, or wonder. Since intrinsic value also refers to the actual, it is possible that aesthetic experience is intrinsically valuable.

But we have tarried long enough, poring over the old world-historical atlases. We have heard rumors that a neglected port is worth visiting. We have checked those rumors and found them worth heeding. We have debated the options once again in general terms. And we have drifted off shore, hearing, from shore to ship, Whitehead's account of the lay of the land. It is about time that we steamed ahead, approached a landing, made fast and disembarked. The natives claim that their exotic treasure is found in present experience. So we must explore the contours of present experience, using Whitehead as our interpreter.

In a moment of present experience, the initial phase is always one of receptiveness. There is a gathering in of data from the past world. One is confronted with a particular panorama. He receives light waves from clouds, barren hills, a lone, gnarled tree on the hills, a scrap of newspaper blowing ten feet in front of him; he receives light waves even from the rims of his glasses and a part of his nose. Also, he is struck with sound waves, of wind blowing through dry weeds, of his own breathing, of the pulse in his ear. He tastes grit in the air, as well as tobacco on his breath. He smells the weeds, as well as his clothes. He feels the wind, as well as the press of his billfold in his pocket. This huge complexity of data is felt physically, from the physical signals sent out by objects in the world. What is felt is the reality that has immediately preceded the subject now feeling it.

A feeling of reality is neither true nor false, neither good nor evil: it simply is. Reality is the world of the past many, as it confronts and gives content to the one, the subject, in the initial phase of its development in a particular moment. To a degree those feelings of reality limit what the world has given it. Relativity is at work; the subject to a degree is what it is because of its relations with its past. And the subject physically feels the world from a particular standpoint. If the subject had been two feet to the right, his perspective and what he would have taken from the world would have been different. In the case cited above, he would have seen the panorama from a little different angle; he might not have seen the scrap of newspaper.

This cannot be the whole story of present experience, however. We know that the observer of the panorama can respond, somewhat freely, to the felt reality of the panorama in a number of ways. He can imagine building a house on the hill; he can pull a Baby Ruth from his pocket and tune his transistor radio to the Everly Brothers; he can pick up the scrap of newspaper; he can turn his back to the scene and walk to town; or he can meditate and wait till sunset. It must be acknowledged that something happens between the observer's reception of reality and his response to that reality.

The observer's response can be individual because he has the capacity to suggest to himself an individual interpretation of reality, which he can accept or reject. There are three phases then: the physically felt reality, the interpretation of that reality, and the final response which concludes whether the individual will deal with reality in terms of the interpretation or not. Eventually, of course, the observer must accept some interpretation. At the least, the interpretation is a determination to concentrate on only a few of the sense data he is receiving. He cannot possibly attend simultaneously to the thousand pieces of sense data. He must abstract from the welter of data a few data that seem interrelated. He is almost sure to neglect the light waves from the rims of his glasses and from the tip of his nose, and the sound waves from his breathing and his pulse. He might concentrate on the scrap of paper blowing over the fields. He might focus on the gnarled tree on the barren hill. Such concentration is itself an interpretation and it occurs by mental feelings. The subject abstracts, from the initial physical data, certain qualitative properties, like the color and shape of the paper, or the colors and shapes of the tree on the hill. While the initial physical reception of data from the world can be called reality, the mental reactions to this reality can be called appearance. Physical feelings of reality lack definiteness and clarity. They give to the subject a "vague totality," [13] which is unconscious or barely conscious. Mental feelings of appearance are definite and clear. Appearance is an interpretation of reality, suggested to the subject. Appearance utilizes a measure of freedom; that is one reason why one's responses to the same reality can differ—one can choose to concentrate on one set of data rather than another, for example.

In order to illustrate the two fundamental aspects of experience, physical feelings of reality and mental feelings of appearance, we have cited a simplified case. We have talked about sense perception, in which a given reality can be dealt with in terms of various appearances. Such appearances "symbolize" felt reality, through the natural symbols of sense perception. Appearances can also symbolize felt reality in terms of conventional symbols, like language and music. Appearances which symbolize felt reality are related to felt reality by what Whitehead calls symbolic reference. Reality also can be dealt with in a more sophisticated way. The subject can receive from reality theories, or propositions. And the subject can mentally feel propositions by "propositional feelings."

Before analyzing symbolic reference and propositions, we should comment on the relation of reality and appearance to aesthetics. Aesthetic experience, or beauty, occurs whenever there is a contrast between reality, or how the individual physically receives his past, and appearance, or how an individual mentally construes his past. By "contrast" we mean to indicate not a contradiction, but a divergence or a difference; for example, we have discussed the divergence between the physically felt, real panorama and the interpretation of the panorama in appearance.[14] This contrast takes place wholly within the moment of present experience. It occurs in the time that is present and in the place that is experience; it is completely within what is actual. Thus, aesthetic contrast occurs totally within the context appropriate for intrinsic value. More positively, the experience of this contrast between appearance and reality is satisfying; it is what gives zest to experience; it is what makes life adventurous.

That aesthetic experience can be an immediate satisfaction is apparent in Whitehead's discussions of art. Art, as Whitehead uses the term,[15] is beauty that is created intentionally, or purposefully. And Whitehead says that art provides for importance in present experience, for art

> is the adaptation of immediate Appearance for immediate Beauty. Art neglects the safety of the future for the gain of the present. In so doing it is apt to render its Beauty thin. But after all, there must be some immediate harvest. The good of the Universe cannot lie in indefinite postponement. The Day of Judgment is an important notion; but that Day is always with us. . . . Art's business is to render the Day of Judgment a success, now.[16]

Beauty that is created unintentionally, with no aim at purposeful adaptation, can also provide this immediate harvest. Beauty, the experience of the contrast between appearance and reality, whether purposeful or not purposeful, provides immediate satisfaction. So Whitehead says that individuals find zest, or the enjoyment of freedom, "by finding some contrast between Appearance resulting from the operations of the mental pole and the inherited realities of the physical pole." [17]

Can this definition of beauty be applied to common examples of aesthetic experience? Think of the panorama described earlier. What if the observer were to concentrate on the scrap of newspaper? He would see the physically felt, real panorama in terms of an appearance in which the scrap of newspaper was of central importance. The interpreted view in terms of the appearance would contrast with the vaguely felt reality. His experience of the contrast might be heightened if he were to interpret the scene as the intrusion of a human artifact (the newspaper) into a stark, natural, wilderness; this more imaginative appearance might contrast more vividly with the vague and massive panorama. The contrast would ask the question, What if this given reality is interpreted as a scene of man's intrusion into nature? Or what if the observer were to concentrate on the gnarled tree on the barren hill? Again, simply this focus would create an appearance that would contrast with the vague totality of physically felt reality. One might photograph the panorama, centering and focusing on the tree. The photograph could ask the question, What if the total scene, which one knows existed in reality when the photograph was taken, were interpreted so that the tree on the hill were of predominant importance? Or the contrast might be heightened if one were to entitle the picture "Loneliness."

The appearance would be more precisely interpreted and would contrast more vividly with the physically felt reality. Now we are contending that it is just such contrasts in the moment of experience that make for aesthetic experience. But such cursory illustrations can raise more questions than they resolve. So we will attempt to provide greater clarity by introducing the classifications of symbolic reference and propositional feelings.

Think of a light show. There are colored strobe lights on a rock group; the volume of the music is greatly amplified. The physical signals sent out by the performance on the stage induces physical feelings of brightly colored figures flashing between interruptions of darkness and emitting throbbing, pounding sounds. But the audience mentally interprets this chaos to construe an appearance that differs from their physical feelings. At least the audience imagines that the musicians are not themselves brightly colored, their movement is not staccato, and their instruments themselves are not throbbing and pounding. Part of the aesthetic value of the experience of such a light show would lie in the sense of the contrast between the chaotic reality and the coherent appearance of ordinary boys with accouterments.

This exemplifies symbolic reference depending on sense perception. Sense perception occurs when there is a causal relation between the felt reality and the appearance. In Whitehead's words, "The sensa derived from bodily activities in the past are precipitated upon the regions in the contemporary world." [18] The appearance of ordinary boys playing their instruments is caused by sensa from the realities of the past.[19] The light and sound waves from the past physically affect the eyes and ears, and these in turn affect the nerves and the brain, so that there is the mental appearance of seeing and hearing a performance, and this appearance is precipitated on the world. The "symbol" is the appearance; the "meaning" of the symbol is the reality to which the subject says the symbol refers;[20] the "symbolic reference" is the connection that says: this symbol refers to such and such a meaning. Symbolic reference comments on the appearance (symbol) by saying that it refers to some reality (meaning). So the light show is a case of symbolic reference depending on sense perception. It is a case of symbolic reference because it involves a reference from appearance to reality; it depends on sense perception because the sense data of reality caused the appearance.

But what happens when someone who is attending his first performance of a light show says to himself, "Ah, that's called a light show"? Admittedly, there is the reality of the light show and there is the appearance, which interprets the reality as a "light show." And, granted, the reality of the sense data cause the appearance of the words. But the nature of the causation is different from the causation in sense perception. With sense perception there is a natural causation that involves limited choice; any observers of a light show at any time would experience the appearance of certain colors, certain shapes, a certain frequency of interruptions of light, and a certain volume of sound. But the naming of a reality involves an almost unlimited choice as to what that name, or appearance, will be. When light shows were first invented, they could have been dubbed "light scene," or "light-sound scene," or "jangle bangles." There is nothing about a real light show that necessarily evokes the phrase l-i-g-h-t s-h-o-w; in France what we call a light show might get a French name. The reality of the light show has come to be related to a particular word, although it could just as well have been related to another; so the causal relation is determined, at a particular point in time, by a choice. When this choice is socially agreed upon, so that most people in a community know that the symbol refers to a particular meaning, then the causal relation between the symbol and the meaning is a social convention. Once this choice has become a social convention, there is a real causal relation; for example, the reality of a light show in the United States necessarily evokes the symbol "light show." And the symbol "light show," through symbolic reference, must refer to the reality, the meaning, of a light show. Whitehead says [21] that this arbitrary connection between meaning and symbol depends on subjective form, or how the reality is felt and how the word is felt. The reality and the word come to be felt with the same tone of feeling. In the case of the light show, it could be said that both come to be felt with a certain noisy, psychedelic tone. Once this identity of tone is established, the causal relation is fixed. So one sees a light show and thinks the word "light show." Or one hears the word "light show" and conjures up an appearance of a light show.

While the causal relation in the symbolic reference of

sense perception is natural, the causal relation in the symbolic reference that involves an arbitrary stipulation is conventional. This latter form of symbolic reference predominates in particular functions of language, music, and ceremony. For example, patriotic music is important not so much for its internal form as for its reference. But that reference is arbitrary and conventional. There is no necessary and natural causal relation between the social, cultural, political, and geographic reality of a nation and the notes and forms of patriotic music about the nation. However, through arbitrary conventional stipulation, certain music felt with a subjective tone of pomp, circumstance, and arrogance has come to refer to one's real nation. The identity of subjective tone, between the feeling of one's real nation and the appearance of patriotic music, has come to make for a conventional causal relation between the two. So one can think of the reality of his nation and then find himself whistling a patriotic tune. And by symbolic reference, it is said that the symbol, which is the tune, refers to the meaning of the real nation.[22]

The aesthetic value of this conventionally based symbolic reference also depends on the vividness of the contrast between the appearance (the symbol) and the reality (the meaning) referred to by the appearance. Oddly, the most significant contrasts might arise when the symbolic reference is incorrect—in the sense that the reality, or the meaning, of the symbolic reference is somehow other than the meaning conventionally associated with the symbol. If one were to call his decrepit car his bicycle, there might be aesthetic merit in such symbolic reference.

When members of the ecological movement sing songs like "America the Beautiful," there may be in their minds a vivid and aesthetically fertile contrast between the appearance of the song and the reality of the nation. When incense, a symbol usually associated with ecclesiastical ritual, is used to refer to the reality of a pot party, there may be for some observers an aesthetically potent contrast.

We have very briefly described the relations of appearance and reality in terms of two forms of symbolic reference, and have attempted to indicate how these relations can involve aesthetic experience. There is, at least, one other major form of relation between appearance and reality which has aesthetic significance.

We are referring to the use of propositions. This use can be illustrated by some comments on the reading of a novel. Certainly, the ocular experience of reading a novel involves the symbolic reference of sense perception; but this sense perception involves very little aesthetic contrast. After you learn enough about reading to see the letters as words, rather than to see pages and margins and your desk, the reference from the focusing on words in appearance to the printed page involves little contrast. Of course, there can be some aesthetic contrast when you are first learning to speed-read, or when you are reading a book with illustrations, or when there are frequent tears and smudges. But sense perception is not at the heart of the aesthetic worth of a novel. Nor does that heart lie in the symbolic reference involving conventional symbols. Yet, the meaning of words depends on such symbolic reference; you see the letters c-a-t and you are able to associate that printed reality with an appearance meaning a small furry animal. After you learn to read, the reference from such appearances to such printed realities involves little contrast and little aesthetic excitement.

A novel is aesthetically valuable because it asks, What if you interpret the kinds of things that are being dealt with in the novel the way the novel interprets them? And the reader reacts to the novel by asking himself, Is that novel's interpretation of those things which I have consciously or unconsciously known about in other connections viable and interesting?

As you read the novel, you receive its physical data physically. With the natural causality of symbolic reference, you perceive the words; and with the conventional causality of symbolic reference, you understand the words. But what you physically receive from the book is not limited to data enabling sense perception and recognition of word meanings. Dependent on this data, but in addition to it, is a physical indication of how the words interrelate with each other, how they participate in a coherent structure. This structure is not simply invented by the reader; he receives a physical indication of it from the physical book. In short, there is in the book a physical indication of a theory, or a proposition, organizing the book. You feel this physical indication physically. And you go on to abstract from your physical feelings of the proposition a mental feeling of the proposition. This is how you interpret the proposition in appearance; Whitehead calls this mental feeling of the proposition a "propositional feeling." The reader's first task is to construe a propositional feeling that corresponds to the proposition as it is physically felt. If the reader understands the novel, if he reads it truthfully, as it "should be read," he will experience a correspondence between his explicit interpretation of the proposition and the proposition as it is dimly and vaguely bodied forth in his physical feelings of the novel. Aesthetic experience in the reading of a novel includes physical feelings of data other than the data of the novel. The reader carries with himself a legacy of common interpretations that concern the same things the novel's proposition concerns. The aesthetic experience in dealing with a novel comes when the reader contrasts his propositional feelings of the novel's proposition with his physical feelings of other relevant propositions.

The novel *Moby Dick* embodies a proposition: Evil should be interpreted in terms of the particular whale hunt for Moby Dick. The novel is experienced aesthetically when the reader asks himself, How does my propositional feeling of the proposition in *Moby Dick* contrast with other physically felt and commonly experienced interpretations of evil?

This assessment of the aesthetic experience of reading a novel can be amplified by a description of Whitehead's definition of propositions. A proposition has two parts. First, there are the facts that are being dealt with in the proposition; Whitehead calls these logical subjects. In the case of *Moby Dick* the logical subjects are the phenomena of evil. Second, there is the structuring of the facts that are being dealt with; Whitehead calls this the predicate of the proposition. In the case of *Moby Dick* the predicate is the structuring configured by a particular whale hunt. Whitehead says that a proposition is a tale "that perhaps might be told about particular actualities." [23]

When you read *Moby Dick* you first attempt to interpret in appearance the proposition as it seems to be in the physically felt book. You attempt to predicate the logical subjects as the novel predicates them; you attempt to interpret the phenomena of evil in the guise of a whale hunt, just as the book has done. This propositional feeling of the book's proposition is then contrasted to physical feelings of common interpretations of evil in reality. These physical feelings of reality are usually dim, unorganized, and barely conscious or even unconscious. Often the reader is unaware of any comparison between his propositional feelings of the proposition in Moby Dick and his physical feelings of common interpretations of evil. Instead, he simply asks himself if *Moby Dick* makes sense. Nevertheless, the juxtaposition of the two kinds of interpretations of evil, the propositional feeling of the novel's proposition and the physical feeling of common interpretations of evil, are the factors in the aesthetic contrast. If there is a vivid contrast between the appearance and the reality, there is aesthetic experience. [24]

For the subject experiencing it, the proposition is an object in his immediate past. For the reader the novel is such an object. For the conductor the musical composition is such an object; for the audience the musical performance is such an object. Although we are dealing in aesthetics, there is no reason to limit propositions to the fine arts. Anything that comments on certain facts in an interpretative way can function as a proposition: a political speech, an academic hypothesis, a scientific theory, a note a mother might leave for a child, a joke, a physical gesture, and, as we will see later, a religious proceeding or ceremony. The proposition is physically embodied in the book, the sheet music, the sounds of an orchestra, a speech, a lecture, etc. But, as an active interpretation of certain facts, it is actual only as it is felt by a subject.[25] A book, forgotten on a shelf, is paper and ink; it becomes an actual suggestion about how certain things might be interpreted only when it is read. Also, it should be noted that the aesthetic experience of the contrast between propositional feelings and feelings of reality is urgent because it seeks a decision. In aesthetic experience the subject is asking, Shall I see things as the propositional feelings suggest or as common feelings of reality suggest? That question seeks a resolution in decision. If the subject accepts the proposition, he decides to interpret reality as the proposition has suggested; then the subject's interpretation of reality is transformed, and he no longer interprets reality as he formerly did. But if the subject rejects the proposition, he decides to interpret reality as he interpreted it prior to his entertainment of the proposition. However, his interpretation of reality will be at least slightly modified; he will know that his interpretation excludes the particular interpretation proposed by the proposition.

These comments on the actuality of propositions and on the kinds of decisions reached about propositions can be illustrated by some hypotheses about listening to the music of J. S. Bach. That music, whether existing in black and white on a sheet of music or existing in the moment of its live performance, is a proposition awaiting a reader or an audience. As a proposition it proposes certain harmonies and progressions of certain notes; the harmonies and progressions proposed are the predicate and the notes so predicated are the logical subjects. The proposition, as an active interpretation, does not assume actuality until it is felt as the datum for a propositional feeling and until that propositional feeling, as an appearance, is contrasted with reality. Now the kind of contrast felt and the kind of decision reached depend on the training and concerns of the listener. For the very esoteric listener, for one who believes that the music should be heard for the pure musical statement, the contrast may be felt as the juxtaposition between Bach's arrangement of notes, and alternative arrangements of notes, as they are known in the listener's reality. But for one who listens to music for its comment on life, the logical subjects (the notes) will represent the many facts of the past world. For this listener the contrast will be experienced as the juxtaposition between Bach's arrangement of notes, as they represent a very ordered and rational form of life, and forms of life as they are bluntly experienced as real for the listener. For this listener, Bach's music may offer a vivid contrast with chaotic forms of contemporary life. Very different contrasts might be evoked by the more violent and chaotic music of such composers as Hindemith, Honegger, or Schönberg. But, in all instances, it is the entertainment of the contrast between the appearance and reality which constitutes the aesthetic experience. After experiencing the aesthetic contrast, the subject decides to what extent he shall accept or reject the musical proposition.

It should be made clear that to entertain the contrast suggested by a proposition is not necessarily to judge that the proposition is true. A proposition is correctly judged as true when it conforms to reality. Now it is conceivable that a proposition might evoke an appearance that is both false, in that it does not conform to reality, and aesthetically satisfying because it exists in vivid contrast with reality. For example, in October of 1966 Senator George Aiken proposed that the United States extricate itself from the Vietnam War in the following way: Let the United States declare itself the victor and leave. The proposition was false. The accepted political definition said we would be the victors when the Communists were licked. In 1966 the Communists were not licked. There existed significant contrast between Aiken's proposition regarding victory and the accepted (real) definition of victory. Many people found that interesting. Some accepted it even though, with regard to the accepted definition, it was false. Then some people, having redefined victory, started saying that we really had won, in that we had given the South Vietnamese respite and fortification, and that was all we ever had any business offering them in the first place. Their view of the Vietnam War was altered and they said, "Now, let's leave." [26]

That a proposition might both be false and evoke a

vivid contrast between appearance and reality might seem obvious. The harder question might be, How can a proposition be true and at the same time evoke a vivid contrast between appearance and reality? How can a propositional feeling that *conforms* to feelings of reality *contrast* with feelings of reality? Whitehead does not seem altogether clear on this matter. But he leaves open at least two possibilities. The first depends on the fact that physical feelings of reality are vague and barely conscious or unconscious. The propositional feeling might evoke to consciousness an interpretation of reality that was not previously explicit but that nevertheless was there implicitly.[27] Second, the proposition might suggest something about reality that was never implicit in reality but that nevertheless is a new and accurate interpretation of reality.[28] In both cases the propositions could be true, because what they say about reality is seen to conform to reality. Also, they could provide contrast, because they compare something that is explicit and obvious to something that is implicit and hidden, and because they say something about reality that is not even implicit in given reality. Propositions of science can be like either of these cases; they can be true and at the same time contrast with accepted understandings of reality.

To this point we have briefly and superficially given our rendition of what seems to be the theory of aesthetic experience implicit in the writings of Alfred North Whitehead. Beauty exists in the present experience of the contrast between appearance and reality.

Whatever in the past world causes that experience—whether it be sense data causing the appearance of symbols or propositions causing propositional feelings—that is the aesthetic object. That object is beautiful.[29] That object does not possess beauty itself; it does not contain actual, presently experienced aesthetic value. But it is called beautiful because it possesses the potentiality of engendering actual beauty in later subjects. Hence, a novel or a painting is not the location of beauty itself; but they may be beautiful if they have the potential to engender beauty.

However, at this point a problem can be anticipated. For because reality is in process, it is quite possible that a novel or a painting which once evokes an appearance that contrasts with reality as it is then known might later fail to evoke an appearance that contrasts with reality as it has later become. As reality changes, the potentiality for objects to evoke an appearance that contrasts with reality can change. What was once beautiful can cease to be beautiful, and what was once not beautiful can become beautiful. At the time of their publication, Jules Verne's *Twenty Thousand Leagues Under the Sea* and *From the Earth to the Moon* embodied propositions that could induce appearances in the reader which contrasted with commonly experienced reality. But commonly experienced reality has changed, and the contrast between the appearance induced by those novels and today's reality (of underwater and space technology) is smaller than it was when the novels were written. If those novels were written today, they might be unpublishable.

They are no longer as beautiful; their capacity to induce aesthetic contrast has diminished. This is an instance of loss of contrast through vagueness. A vague relation between appearance and reality occurs when appearance and reality are very similar. Old jokes, which are part of everyone's experience, are no longer funny. Conversely, with the passage of time reality can change, so that an appearance that once contrasted with reality as it was formerly experienced will seem irrelevant to reality as it has come to be experienced. Again, the object that causes that appearance will no longer be as beautiful as it once was. Some argue that the music of J. S. Bach has lost aesthetic merit for this reason. They contend that the progression of life has come to be so dominated by chaos and irrationality that the ordered and rational form of life represented by Bach's music has become irrelevant; the appearance generated by that music has lost contact with presently experienced reality and, consequently, cannot enter into significant contrast with reality. To take Bach's music seriously, except for esoteric reasons of historical interest, becomes a belief in a lie, or worse, a belief in a silly, irrelevant lie. This is an instance of a loss of contrast through triviality. Triviality occurs when reality has become so dissimilar to appearance as to be irrelevant to appearance. "Incompatibility has predominated over contrast." [30] A joke that is out of touch with reality might be thought of as obscene. But it is also possible that an appearance, as it relates to a changing reality, can move from vagueness or triviality to contrast. Then an object that once was not beautiful can become beautiful. For example, it often happens that an appearance evoked by the works of a good artist deviates so radically from reality, as the layman knows it, that the layman will think that the appearance has no relevance to reality and, hence, no contrast with reality and, hence, no aesthetic merit. But through time the layman's perceptions of reality might change sufficiently so that the appearance comes to have relevance and contrast to reality and, consequently, aesthetic merit for the layman. A trivial relation would become a significant contrast. French impressionism was given a poor reception in the 1890's. The bright colors and the spotty dispersion of paints simply violated accepted norms. Apparently few people saw the new school as embodying a significant interpretation of reality. But now, in the second half of the 1900's, very big money is given for the originals, Hollywood and Kirk Douglas make *Lust for Life* (a biographical movie of Vincent van Gogh), and there are prints of impressionist paintings in the living rooms of the bourgeoisie. It is possible that this happened because the layman's perceptions of reality changed.

In short, whether or not something is beautiful depends on what happens in reality. This conclusion presupposes a particular understanding of aesthetic contrast; it presupposes a criterion for aesthetic contrast. Whitehead calls a proper aesthetic contrast a harmony. Harmony requires a "combination of width and narrowness." [31] "All aesthetic experience is feeling arising out of contrast under identity." [32] Optimal beauty exists where the fullest possible contrast between appearance and reality (thus avoiding vagueness) is contained in a unified experience (thus avoiding triviality). The greater the contrast within identity, the greater the beauty. Whitehead adds that the aesthetic experience is enhanced if the things commented upon in an aesthetic contrast are felt to be important.[33]

III

It would be nice if, just for a moment, we could stop probing and picking our way through subterranean depths, and haul ourselves up into the glare of ordinary life. After all, we descended into that metaphysical cellar, not because we liked damp and murky places; we burrowed down because we wanted to learn about the ground on which we stood. What is it about the ground on which we live that makes life worth living? Can that ground support life? In particular, is there some way in which it can be said that there is intrinsic value, experience useful simply for being had, in life? In search of an answer we crawled down through separate shafts into the separate chambers of truth, goodness, and the experience of the holy. And we have just followed Whitehead down into the chambers of beauty.

But now, if you have a lungful of fresh air and a little warmth from the sun, we should go down again. We do this at the risk of aggravating intellectual arthritis and encouraging the stiffening that comes with it. Perhaps you could be persuaded to descend if I told you that

Whitehead has hollered up some news: The chambers are connected down here! Beauty is connected with goodness, truth, and the experience of the holy!

Beauty and Goodness

The subject is directed by two aims, an aesthetic aim and an ethical aim. Whitehead says, "The subjective aim, whereby there is origination of conceptual feelings, is at intensity of feeling (*a*) in the immediate subject, and (*b*) in the *relevant* future." [34] The subjective aim at intensity of feeling in the immediate subject is correlative to the aesthetic aim; it aims to attain beauty in the only actuality that there is for the subject—the present experience of that subject. The subjective aim at intensity of feeling in the relevant future is correlative to what could be called the ethical aim; it aims to attain beauty in the nonactual future by making the present, actual subject a beautiful object for the future. The aesthetic aim is directed toward adapting appearance so that it contrasts with reality and gives present aesthetic satisfaction. While the aesthetic aim alone has the virtue of being concerned with the realization of beauty in what is actual, it can be dangerous when it disregards all consideration for the ethical aim. In the evening the drunk might proclaim his concern for present beauty, but in the morning he might think he had damaged his future. On the other hand, one who is dominated by the ethical aim is insufficiently concerned with beauty in what is actual—present experience. A miser might argue that he is working for future beauty, but on his deathbed he might think he had continually damaged his actual present. Often, however, the two aims are compatible. Sometimes the best way to prepare for the beauty of friendship tomorrow is to enjoy it today.

Beauty and goodness, then, can be related as the aesthetic aim and the ethical aim are related. While neither should be dominant, it is not accurate to think of them as having equivalent importance. Again, beauty seems to be of paramount importance. First, the experience of beauty is an experience of intrinsic value in what is actual, while the experience of goodness is an experience of instrumental value for what is the nonactual future. Second, aesthetic considerations have infected the ethical orientation, for the aim of ethics is not toward some classical ethical value, some ethical law, etc., but toward the experience of future beauty. Third, often the present will be good or beautiful for the future because the present subject is in the act of experiencing beauty. The scholar who enjoys his work is usually more creative for the future. The teacher who is playful is usually more effective with his students. The friend who likes you is usually more helpful to you. Those who are adept at experiencing present aesthetic satisfaction are usually ethically effective.

Beauty and goodness also can be related in terms of their contribution to the evolution of life. Usually, to have an aim in life is to intend that life be made better. To want to make life better is to intend that life be more than simply processive; it is to want the process to move upward. Beauty is the effort to make life better now;

goodness is the effort to make life better in the future.

Evolution, as it is supported by beauty and goodness, is met by a counter movement. While the reality of living things is animated by the urge to evolve up, to live better,[35] physical reality is devolving down, undergoing entropy. This is hardly an original insight, but Whitehead puts it nicely:

> If we survey the world as a physical system determined by its antecedent states, it presents to us the spectacle of a finite system steadily running down— losing its activities and its varieties. . . . But there is in nature some tendency upwards, in a contrary direction to the aspect of physical decay. In our experience we find appetition, effecting a final causation towards ideal ends which lie outside the mere physical tendency. In the burning desert there is appetition towards water, whereas the physical tendency is towards increased dryness of the animal body. The appetition towards esthetic satisfaction by some enjoyment of beauty is equally outside the mere physical order.[36]

Process pursues two courses: decadence and emergence. Life process must fight to emerge, or it will be sucked down in the decadence of physical process. It is impossible to hold things on a level: "Advance or Decadence are the only choices offered to mankind. The pure conservative is fighting the essence of the universe." [37] Sheer repetition will lead to boredom, and boredom will lead to fatigue, and fatigue will lead to decadence.

The aim toward beauty, whether it is the aesthetic aim or the ethical aim, is the aim toward emergence. This aim must include the concern for novelty, for emergence occurs only when the subject's interpretation is to some extent novel. It is novelty in the imagined appearance which allows the appearance to deviate from the given reality. Whitehead says:

> A race preserves its vigour so long as it harbors a real contrast between what has been and what may be; and so long as it is nerved by the vigour to adventure beyond the safeties of the past. Without adventure civilization is in full decay.[38]

The experience of beauty is the suggestion that a quantum leap be made from what was, to the novelty of what is mentally imagined now; and therein is beauty's contribution to actual emergence. Ethics seeks the means that should be adopted now, so that quantum leaps of beauty will be more likely in the future; and therein is ethics' contribution to potential emergence. Morality is action in accordance with such means. Whitehead says, "The effect of the present on the future is the business of morals." [39] He also says, "The real world is good when it is beautiful." [40] And, as we have learned, something is beautiful when it has the potential for promoting the experience of beauty in the future.

Now the unique significance of ethics is that it sustains an awareness of the crisis of life process through time. Ethics warns: Prepare for future beauty and future emergence or decadence will ensue. Ethics is conscious that "the teleology of the Universe is directed to the production of Beauty." [41] And with this in mind, ethics has the right to reject present beauty that might inhibit future beauties. The aesthetic aim is like a child who wants to play into the night, with the immediate joys of aesthetic satisfaction and the rewards of present accomplishments. Ethics calls the child to bed so that it will be able to play tomorrow. Pollution is an ethical problem. To pollute is to countenance the beauties of profligacy today and to destroy the possibilities for beauty tomorrow.

Beauty and Truth

Truth can be related to beauty as both an aid and an impediment. Truth exists where appearance conforms to reality; an appearance is adjudged true when it describes accurately some aspect of reality, as it is physically felt. If one says, "There are two chairs in front of me," and if this interpretation of what is before him corresponds to his physical sense impressions, then the statement is true.

Truth can aid beauty by keeping it somewhat honest. Or, as Whitehead says, truth is "akin to cleanliness—namely, the removal of dirt, which is unwanted irrelevance. . . . Falsehood is corrosive." [42] Most of the time, beauty that greatly deviates from truth is irrelevant. Usually, when appearance is untrue to reality, it is so foreign to reality that it loses touch with reality; then it is unlikely that there can be significant contrast between appearance and reality; and without that contrast there is no aesthetic experience, or beauty. The appearance would be trivial. In addition, if an appearance that is untrue to reality is accepted as true, and if interpretations of reality are altered accordingly, then the moral effect of that acceptance sometimes can be destructive.[43] For example, the call for violent revolution can be a suggestion untrue to the conventional and established procedures for social change. Listening to the rhetoric of revolution can be an aesthetic experience of contrast in the moment. But if the revolutionary suggestion is accepted as a true reading of the situation, and if action is taken that ignores the conventional procedures, those conventional procedures may well crush the revolution. Or, to take a less relevant example, a child might acquire aesthetic satisfaction one night from hearing the story of Dumbo, the elephant who could fly by flapping his big ears. But if the child accepted that interpretation of elephants as true, the effect of the story might not be beauteous. The next day on safari the child might try to outrun a rampaging elephant, rather than climb a tree, because he would assume that the elephant would fly up to get him if he climbed a tree.

But a continuous allegiance to truth can impede beauty. An excessive concern with truth can foster vagueness, where appearance is excessively similar to reality. And to seek truth alone would be to refuse to entertain appearances that do not conform to reality as it has been physically received. Basically, it would be a commitment to seeing and doing things in the present the way they have been seen and done in the past. But, as we have seen, the conservative, holding the line, leads to decadence. A beauty untruthful to past reality can be helpful, especially in stagnant and sterile situations. Such an untruthful beauty would be a contrast between reality and an appearance that interprets reality in such an unorthodox way that there is discord between that appearance and reality. This discord can promote a vital reassessment of reality. Whitehead says, "Thus the contribution to Beauty which can be supplied by Discord—in itself destructive and evil—is the positive feeling of a quick shift of aim from the tameness of outworn perfection to some other ideal with its freshness still upon it." [44] "Progress is founded upon the experience of discordant feelings." [45] Repeatedly he says that it is more important that a proposition be interesting than that it be true. So it seems proper to conclude that beauty is more important than truth:

> It is evident, however, that the primary function of theories is as a lure for feeling, thereby providing immediacy of enjoyment and purpose.[46]

> In itself, and apart from other factors, there seems to be no special importance about the truth-relation. . . . In other words, a truth-relation is not necessarily beautiful. It may not even be neutral. It may be evil. Thus Beauty is left as the one aim which by its very nature is self-justifying.[47]

Beauty and the Experience of the Holy

Finally, then, what is the relation between the experience of beauty and the experience of the holy? Earlier we argued that the experience of the holy, as it has been described by two major historians of religion, is an experience that refers to something so remote from ordinary experience that it is difficult to understand how that experience could be of intrinsic value. We can note now that Whitehead does not discuss at any length an experience of a holy that is remote. When he does, there is included a sharp rejection of a remote, absolute, transcendent God.[48] Nevertheless, for Whitehead, God is involved in aesthetic experience. But Whitehead thinks of the experience of the holy as the experience of a reality that is close and immanent, rather than remote and transcendent. The role of God, so conceived, is seen through an analysis of appearance.

In our earlier discussion of appearance, in the forms of symbol and propositional feeling, we neglected to emphasize innovation. The persons who first created the light show and Herman Melville, as he wrote *Moby Dick*, were interpreting reality as it had not previously been interpreted. Also, the audience at the light show and the readers of *Moby Dick*, as they dealt with the suggestions of the light show and of *Moby Dick*, added an interpretative twist that was innovative and their own. That is why, for example, different people can find different things in a novel, or why even the same person can find something new each time he rereads the same novel. In short, both the creators and the interpreters of symbols and propositions come to say something about reality that is new, or that was not explicitly clear in reality previously. This innovation is very significant aesthetically, for with it appearance can deviate from reality in a radical way. Without this innovation the subject's interpretation of reality is distinctive only in that it is made

from a particular standpoint and with a particular perspective on reality, and in that it makes certain rough
abstractions from reality—such as choosing to see a pas-
ture as green when in fact it has browns and grays and
other colors in it.[49] While these particular perspectives
on and abstractions about reality make for a certain par-
ticularity of appearance, they do not allow for the introduction of new ideas which can make appearance deviate radically from reality. With genuine innovation the
subject introduces into appearance new qualities—qualities that are partially identical with and partially diverse
from the qualities implicit in initial feelings of reality.
These new qualities are introduced after the qualities
have been mentally abstracted from physical feelings of
reality; also, the new qualities must be relevant to those
abstracted qualities. Whitehead calls this later, secondary
introduction of qualities "conceptual reversion." [50] Conceptual reversion is guided by the aim of attaining a
depth of contrast by introducing relevant diversities.[51]

But the question remains, Where do the qualities introduced by conceptual reversion come from? If the correspondence theory of truth is accepted, this is a necessary
question. Normally, we deem a presently entertained notion true if it corresponds to, or represents, what the case
was in the past. So we have said that an appearance can
be acknowledged as true if it conforms to reality as it is
physically felt. Technically, this means that the qualities
in the appearance should correspond to qualities in the
real object that is being felt. And, where truth is claimed,
it is generally acknowledged that the qualities of the ap-

pearance not only correspond to reality but also are derived in some way from reality. The qualities are abstracted from, or taken from, the real object being felt. But this raises a question. If the correspondence theory of truth holds that true appearances both conform to and are abstracted from reality, to what reality do true novel ideas conform, and from what reality are they abstracted? If, in the moment of its creation, Melville's interpretation of evil was true, to what reality did it conform, and from what reality was it abstracted? If Melville's interpretation was really innovative, it did not correspond to or derive from interpretations in the past —otherwise it would not be innovative. Did Melville's interpretation correspond to and was it derived from a reality not heretofore manifested? This would be to entertain truth of a different order than that discussed previously; previously we were concerned with truth that corresponds to past reality. Here we are discussing truth that corresponds, not to past reality, but to reality that is being discovered and that has not been manifest in the past. The question remains, To what reality does a true novel idea correspond, and from what reality does it originate?

Of course, in certain quarters this question will appear to be silly. In those quarters the counterargument might be that new ideas are simply conjured up, more or less out of one's guts, that one gets a new idea by "just imagining it." It is interesting that this explanation of creativity often comes from empirically-minded people who in all other cases insist that knowledge is knowledge of and from some reality outside the knower—otherwise, you are talking of baseless fantasy. But, at the same time, they can say that a novel idea (new knowledge) is just created—pop!—out of nothing. Is this the one great case of spontaneous generation? Is this a strangely anachronistic faith in the brain's capacity to give birth . . . virginally? Sometimes this theory will be rescued from naïveté by a behavioristic psychological description that might say that an innovation is a possibly fortuitous, but felicitous, occurrence through a synapse in the brain, connecting hitherto unconnected ideas. But how does this work in any given situation? When a movement of thought hits a dead end, it needs just the right new synapse to open the way. How, when there is a huge number of irrelevant synapses, does it happen that one of the few relevant synapses occurs? But if that question were answered, the behaviorist could maintain that innovation, as he understands it, is a humble phenomenon: it is just a new relation of the same old ideas. So, it could be argued, there is no need to talk of the introduction of something brand new. But this is to diminish the importance of relations. If A and B exist apart, that is one thing; if A and B are connected, that involves a relation, which is something new; if A and B are connected in relation Z after having been connected in relation Y, then something new has happened. Mathematics, like sexual intercourse, is a discipline that innovates by creating fresh relations. So to combine old factors in new relations is a dramatic introduction of a new idea. Where does the new idea come from?

Other people, people not inclined to say, "I just imagined it," might say, "A new idea just hit me." They contend that novelty originates not within the self, but from beyond the self. Following this view, Whitehead says:

> The type of Truth required for the final stretch of Beauty is a discovery and not a recapitulation. The Truth that for such extremity of Beauty is wanted is that truth-relation whereby Appearance summons up new resources of feeling from the depths of Reality.[52]

So he contends that novel ideas, or qualities, the qualities introduced by conceptual reversion, come from and refer to "the depths of Reality." This is the truth of a different order, referred to earlier.

But what is meant by "the depths of Reality"? Whatever that depth is, it must serve at least two functions. First, it must present to the subject new possibilities, or qualities. Second, it must present new possibilities that are relevant; then appearance influenced by conceptual reversion can receive possibilities that are relevant in that they are partially identical with and partially diverse from the qualities abstracted from the subject's physical feelings of reality. Do these two functions, which might make innovation possible, place a requirement on any metaphysic? Is there in fact some source and object for new possibilities and some reason for the fact that they are relevant to the subject? Must a metaphysic, accounting for what happens in fact, postulate some answer to these questions? Anyway, Whitehead takes these questions seriously and postulates the existence of God as an answer to these—as well as other—questions. So Whitehead will say:

> Apart from the intervention of God, there could be nothing new in the world, and no order in the world. The course of creation would be a dead level of ineffectiveness, with all balance and intensity progressively excluded by the cross currents of incompatibility.[53]

An understanding of how God might render these services presupposes at least a brief acquaintance with Whitehead's notion of God. Somewhat like any individual, God has three aspects.[54] In any moment an individual has: (1) the character given it by what it receives from the past; (2) the character that develops as it entertains an interpretation of its past in the atomic moment of experience; and (3) the objective character, formed by a concluding decision about how it will interpret the world and how it will, in turn, be as a past object for the future world. The first aspect is similar to what Whitehead calls the primordial nature of God, which is the nature that is presupposed, or given, in any moment. However, its primordial status makes it also dissimilar from other individuals, in that it is the first "given" order in all world process; it comes from no past. It is also eternal, or unchanging through time. It is "the unlimited conceptual realization of the absolute wealth of potentiality." [55] As primordial, God is the repository for all potential qualities, including both those already realized and in actuality, and those still unrealized and potential. Also as primordial, God's conceptual realization of all potentiality provides the conditions under which all process operates; these are conditions of order—virtually equivalent to those fundamental continuities that metaphysics attempts to describe. The second aspect of individuals is similar to what Whitehead calls the consequent nature of God; this concerns God as he, from moment to moment, feels and is affected by the past world. The third aspect is similar to what Whitehead calls the superjective nature of God, or God as he has decided about the world from moment to moment and as he is as a past object for the future world.

It is the superjective nature of God that presents relevant novelties to the subject, making conceptual reversion possible. In conceptual reversion the subject is related to the superjective nature of God as a reality, similar to the way the subject is related to ordinary past realities. The superjective nature of God presents potentialities to subjects, and it can present some potentialities that are implicit in the primordial nature of God but that were not actualized heretofore in the past actual world. In short, the superjective nature can be the source and the object for feelings of novel potentialities. Also, the superjective nature can provide, for the subject, an order of relevance for the novel potentialities.[56] God has felt the past world, through the consequent nature, and has felt it also in terms of the full range and order of potentialities implicit in the primordial nature. So the superjective nature can say, given the past world and given the full range and order of potentials, here is how

certain potentials—including unactualized potentials—
are germane with regard to the past world and for the
subject that is now in process. In short, this order of relevance can make it possible for the subject to entertain
possibilities that are relevant or that are partially identical
with and partially diverse from the qualities previously
abstracted from reality. This divine influence makes possible in the subject an innovative mental appearance
that contrasts significantly with past reality. And this, in
turn, makes possible the aesthetic experience of that contrast. So Whitehead will say:

> The metaphysical doctrine, here expounded, finds
> the foundations of the world in the aesthetic ex-
> perience, rather than—as with Kant—in the cogni-
> tive and conceptive experience. All order is there-
> fore aesthetic order, and the moral order is merely
> certain aspects of aesthetic order. The actual world
> is the outcome of the aesthetic order, and the aes-
> thetic order is derived from the immanence of
> God.[57]

Thus God is the measure of the aesthetic consistency
of the world.[58]

What, then, is the relation between the experience of
innovative beauty and the experience of the holy? The
experience of beauty is the experience of the contrast between appearance and reality. Without novelty in appearance, appearance will basically conform to and be
true to past reality; but there will be little contrast between appearance and reality, and, hence, little or no
beauty. It is the presence of novelty in appearance that

makes both for significant contrast between appearance and reality, and for significant beauty. But we have learned that novelty occurs through conceptual reversion, and that conceptual reversion is a feeling of the superjective nature of God.[59] Therefore, the superjective nature of God is experienced as the novelty that gives significant contrast and makes significant beauty possible. In short, the experience of God is the experience of novelty. So the relation of the experience of the holy to the experience of beauty is identical to the relation of the experience of novelty to the totality of the experience of beauty. Novelty makes appearance deviate from reality so that an aesthetic contrast arises. In other words, the experience of the holy alters appearance, making beauty possible.

Some theorists of creativity will talk of the "Aha!" experience. This occurs when, after repeated descriptions and interpretations of reality, a novel factor is introduced into appearance which causes appearance to contrast felicitously with reality. The introduction of this novelty is greeted with the reaction, "Aha!" It is conjectured that the Old Testament designation of God, Yahweh, is possibly an onomatopoeic rendering of the involuntary inhalation that often accompanies awe: "Yaaaa!" Could these be analogous responses to the holy?

Now if this assessment of the role of the experience of the holy in aesthetic experience is accepted, several theological implications are immediately obvious. The first implication is that God is known usually in what is called general revelation, rather than in special revelation.[60] God is not often encountered in extraordinary psychological states (a la *mysterium tremendum*), or as one who is remote (a la wholly other), or in a few special moments of a special history (a la *Heilsgeschichte*). But he is encountered in all ordinary aesthetic experience; and aesthetic experience is a form of general revelation because it is not confined to any particular history and is available generally in life. The second implication is that the experience of the holy is always relative to the individual experiencing it or to the culture for which it is of ultimate significance. Conceptual reversion must present to the emerging subject a novel idea that is relevant to the subject's view of reality, where relevance means that the novel idea will in part diverge from and in part identify with the subject's view of reality. Hence, the novelty, or the experience of God, is relative to the subject or to the culture for which it is of ultimate significance. But an experience of God relevant to one subject or culture might well be irrelevant to another subject or culture; it might not be productive of an appearance that would meaningfully contrast with the other individual's or culture's views of reality. Hence, no experience of God—including that mediated by Jesus—can be final or absolute, or relevant to all places and times. However, this would not mean that any individual's or any culture's experiences of God would be isolated from any other individual's or any other culture's experiences of God. There is no need to envision a solipsistic relativism, where no one shares what the other has because everything, including the experience of the holy, is peculiarly relative to each individual or culture, with the result that interrelation between individuals and cultures is impossible. For each is viewing, from his particular standpoint on reality, the same absolute order: the primordial nature of God—as it is manifest in the superjective nature of God. So there would be a basis for a commonality of all experiences of God, and a basis for interrelation on religious matters. Third, while truth may remind the subject of past experiences of God and while morality may prepare for future experiences of God, the aesthetic contrast provides the situation for the actual experience of God.

But we are verging on theology proper. We have seen that within the metaphysical framework provided by Whitehead beauty can be related to goodness and truth and the experience of the holy. We have concluded by maintaining that aesthetic experience, while it provides the situation in which the holy is experienced, nevertheless is dependent on the experience of the holy. We have followed Whitehead in the hair-raising enterprise of positing a God. We would like to have avoided such a dubious conjecture if it had seemed possible. Certainly, any notion supported with such scanty evidence as supports a God hypothesis should be avoided if possible. And, certainly, we could have stopped short of talking about God. But then how could the introduction of relevant novelties have been explained? Since we saw no alternative but to introduce a God hypothesis, we should probably stick with it and move on to theological analysis.

IV. APPENDIX: RELEVANT SCHOLARSHIP

In the interest of making the foregoing analysis of Whitehead's thought more readable, we have omitted mention of relevant scholarly writings. It is a fact of life that certain forms of persuasion seem to require at least a passing comment on scholarship. So we will attempt just that—a passing comment.

In the theology and the philosophy of religion that has been influenced by the process philosophy of Alfred North Whitehead there has been a strange inattention to the aesthetic dimension in Whitehead's thought. Consequently, there has been little note of the importance that aesthetics might have for such theology and philosophy of religion.

In most theology and philosophy of religion influenced by Whitehead primary attention has been given to truth. In most "process theology," that is, theology influenced by process philosophy, this attention has taken the form of an empiricist, or historicist, concentration on Jesus of Nazareth. The objective has been to acquire the truth about Jesus and to relate it to Whitehead's philosophical perspective. Some of the theological writings of John B. Cobb, Jr., and Schubert Ogden represent this kind of focus on truth. This preoccupation with truth is most emphatic when each author claims that the revelation of Jesus is "final," or that it is a truth that is unsurpassable.[61] In the philosophy of religion of Charles Hartshorne this preoccupation with truth takes a different form. There a rationalistic quest for truth is enunciated. Hartshorne's primary objective is to describe truths about God as he is eternally absolute.[62]

Now, given this concentration on truth, it is understandable that the aesthetic dimension has been neglected. For we have argued that the aesthetic dimension assumes crucial importance when the processive character of reality has constricted actuality to the moment of present experience. But if truth is of paramount importance, if the task of ascertaining the truth about the Jesus of history or of God as he has been known is the primary concern, then past events take on great value. It can appear that the past is so authoritative that the purpose of life is to understand the past, which is to have the truth. But, as we argued at the opening of this chapter, this seems to deny the processive character of reality—which says that the past is dead and, hence, cannot be of central importance. If the processive character of reality is implicitly denied, there is no particular need to find the aesthetic of crucial importance.

In process theology another note has been sounded. The only man—to my knowledge—to sound that note long and consistently in writing is Bernard E. Meland. He has characterized reality as processive and the direction of the process as emergent; he has characterized God as a good not our own, who fosters life by encouraging fresh insight. And, most important, Meland is skeptical of man's capacity to know the truth. But, for Meland, this is not to be skeptical about man. For man is a physical and wondering being, as well as an intellectual being.

Man emerges when he becomes appreciative, aware, sensitive to the vague indications of significance that undergird him. Although he does not frequently refer to his orientation as aesthetic, it seems that Meland is calling for an aesthetic approach to religious meaning, rather than an empirical or rationalistic approach.[63]

There have been several explicit efforts to point out the aesthetic orientation of Whitehead's thought. Stanley Romaine Hopper has written the definitive essay, showing that the aesthetic emphasis is central to Whitehead's thought, although he does not explain how that emphasis arises from Whitehead's epistemology and metaphysics.[64] But there have been several attempts to explain how, metaphysically and epistemologically, the aesthetic emphasis is important in Whitehead's thought.

The most thorough and noteworthy exposition of the aesthetic orientation and implications of Whitehead's thought is Donald W. Sherburne's *A Whiteheadian Aesthetic*. Recognizing that a philosophical system is judged finally, not on its ability to supply irrefutable proofs, but on its ability to apply to a variety of questions, Sherburne proposes to demonstrate the applicability of Whitehead's system to aesthetic questions and phenomena.[65] Sherburne notes that Whitehead has shown the applicability of his system to religious phenomena, and Edmund Jabez Thompson has shown the applicability of Whitehead's system to moral interests, but that no one, including Whitehead, has shown the applicability of the system to aesthetic questions. So Sherburne is in business. While I do not disagree with

Sherburne's book, page by page, I think several fundamental points are a little off the mark.

1. Throughout the book Sherburne seems to assume that beauty is restricted to art and art is restricted to the fine arts. While it is typical of aesthetics, this reduction seems both unnecessary and un-Whiteheadian. After all, Whitehead was capable of saying that "the teleology of the universe is directed to the production of Beauty." [66] By comparison, art, as Whitehead uses the term, is limited to the "purposeful adaptation of Appearance to Reality." [67] Whitehead repeatedly comments on the comprehensive importance of beauty in all life; it seems unlikely that he would identify all beauty with artistic, or purposefully created, beauty. Nor is there a reason, of which I am aware, to believe that Whitehead restricts art to the fine arts. It is apparent that Whitehead has a broader concept of art when he says: "In short, art is the education of nature. Thus, in its broadest sense, art is civilization." [68] The problem, as I see it, is that Sherburne, by restricting the definition of beauty, restricts the importance that beauty might have for life. The satisfaction derived from aesthetic experience is available to all people in almost all situations.

2. Sherburne says, "It is characteristic of this theory that it pivots about an account of the ontological status of aesthetic objects; this account is the cement that holds together the other elements constitutive of it." [69] Sherburne says that the aesthetic object is a proposition, objectified in a past art work; and he goes on to claim that the account of the aesthetic object is "the essential as-

pect of this aesthetic theory." [70] This seems to be one more case of placing the source of importance in what is nonactual—the nonactuality of a proposition and the nonactuality of the past. I would think that the source of importance and the essential element of a Whiteheadian aesthetic must be in actuality, or present experience. In fact, as what is alone actual, present experience would determine whether something were or were not an art object at all. Also, by identifying art objects with propositions, Sherburne omits consideration of art in symbolic reference—which seems crucial in our account above.[71]

3. Sherburne does allow for "artistic creation" in the present moment of experience. This occurs through what Sherburne calls "horizontal transmutation." He feels that propositional feelings as explicitly described by Whitehead would fail to involve a sensing of the interrelatedness of things.[72] They will only reiterate the simple and obvious factors of reality. So Sherburne proposes "horizontal transmutation" as the procedure whereby a propositional feeling is supplemented by data that are in the subject's feelings of reality, but that are there as dim and unconscious. This introduction of data provides new possibilities for interrelatedness which can make the propositional feeling aesthetically creative. A good artistic creation evokes data and relations not explicitly felt before. The aesthetic creation is then primarily descriptive of the past objective world and is distinctive because it is a new synthesis. And as a *new* synthesis it involves the novelty-producing roles of conceptual reversion and God.

Certainly, the aesthetic creation is important partly because it does involve fresh synthesis. But to concentrate on this as central is, I believe, to neglect the principal implications of originative aesthetic experience, which I have described as the felt contrast between appearance and reality. A concentration on the feeling of the interrelatedness of the past seems to neglect the radicalness of beauty: that it is an experience of the contrast between the reality that is and the appearance that might be. Appearance's divergence from reality and its consequent incitement to reinterpret reality are, in Sherburne, toned down to the level of a fine arts synthesis of implicit factors in reality. Also, it is strange that Whitehead, with all his categories and neologisms, did not see fit to specify a procedure like horizontal transmutation—if it is in fact so central to artistic creation.

These are some of our objections to Sherburne's approach. But the book is valuable and replete with pregnant suggestions pertaining to traditional aesthetic problems.

John Cobb took a crack at defining a Whiteheadian aesthetic in an article in 1957, "Toward Clarity in Aesthetics." [73] He states that the purpose of the essay is to define the aesthetic and the function of the aesthetic; and he concludes the first paragraph by saying, "Successful achievement of these ends should resolve most of the contradictions between aestheticians." [74] Whew.

It seems to me that Cobb begins properly. He says that to be actual is to be involved in experience and that "if whatever is actual has its being in actual occasions, 'the aesthetic' must be sought there." [75] Cobb then turns to the actual and determines that the aesthetic must be in subjective form, or how the subject feels the past. He discusses subjective form in the modes of causal efficacy and of presentational immediacy. An object is aesthetic if it contributes to the form of causal efficacy in such a way that the subject has the possibility of experiencing beauty. But the aesthetic experience itself occurs in the subjective form of presentational immediacy. Where that form includes a complex pattern such that lasting satisfaction results, there is aesthetic experience.

Sherburne discusses Cobb and faults him for being subjectivistic and for failing to specify the objective character of the aesthetic. I would compliment Cobb for his subjectivism, for at least it places the aesthetic in the actual. Since the propositional character of art is so crucial for Sherburne, I should think he would have criticized Cobb for describing a Whiteheadian aesthetic without mentioning propositions.

I do not see how Cobb can place the aesthetic in presentational immediacy, which is mere appearance. Again, I would argue that this misses the radicalness of beauty: that it is an experience of the contrast between the reality that is and the appearance that says what might be, and that, as such, it constitutes an incitement for a reinterpretation of reality.[76]

CHAPTER IV

A THEOLOGY OF BEAUTY

There is a special advantage to working in theology. In most other academic disciplines—especially in the natural sciences—when your hypothesis is not corroborated by the majority of specialists in your field, you are in trouble. After a while you might as well give it up. Although this is generally the rule in theology, there is, in certain instances, another ploy. To make it work, you concentrate on that minor tradition which says, The really authentic religious expression is always unpopular. Abraham believed the strangers when they said he would have a son; old Sarah snickered but later had to own up to being pregnant. Joseph fancied that his many-colored robe indicated a special destiny; his brothers beat him up; years later he watched them lie prostrate before him, begging for food from their brother, who had become prime minister. The prophets made a big point of being both unpopular and right. Jesus preached in his old neighborhood and, when he was denigrated as a mere carpenter's son, he complained that a prophet is without honor in his own country; but the story goes on to say that Jesus did pretty well. One can think of Tertullian, Kierkegaard, and Karl Barth, all examples that encourage the adoption of a position that is out of tune with the times. So in religious thought you do have a second line of defense.

In the history of Christian thought the popular bywords have been peace, communion, stability, continuity, unity. In contemporary theology the popular byword has been love, described by Reinhold Niebuhr as harmony and by Paul Tillich as reunion. This is the popular tradition. The unpopular theme, the minor note, is: commotion. Theology privately plans commotion and religion publicly enacts commotion. Within the Judeo-Christian tradition the development of religious thought and the evolution of religious man is incomprehensible apart from the function of ideas and acts which intentionally engendered commotion. That development and evolution was caused by individuals who promulgated commotion by introducing possibilities so deviant from the norm that they caused strife and enthusiasm. In retrospect it is Abraham, Joseph, the prophets, Jesus, Tertullian, Kierkegaard, and Barth that we honor, not their opponents. But, of course, the popular byword advises, That's enough, no more; now let's get together.

But if I have the choice, I would rather ignore such popular admonitions. Who would not prefer to be allied with Abraham rather than Sarah, with Joseph rather than his big brothers, with the real prophets rather than the false prophets, with Jesus rather than his old neighbors?

So I want to call for more commotion. To do so is merely to accept the implications of aesthetic experience. Aesthetic experience is experience of a contrast in a moment of subjective experience: the contrast between the physical feelings of reality and appearance—which is the mental interpretation of reality proposed by the self to the self in the moment of experience. When the subject entertains the contrast between the feelings of reality and the interpretation proposed by appearance, the subject experiences aesthetic satisfaction. Because appearance does deviate from the accepted, given feeling of reality, the interpretation proposed by appearance can, at times, be evaluated as unkempt and unorthodox; at its extreme the entertainment of the appearance can be censured with the explicatives: Vulgar! Heresy! And because the contrast is fresh and vivid, it is felt with interest, at least, and possibly with real excitement. At its extreme the entertainment of the contrast can be censured with the explicatives: Romantic! Sensational! Such reactions indicate not a serious entertainment of the aesthetic contrast, but its popular and immediate rejection, out of hand. It is condemned because it might incite disunity, turbulence, and change. But it is possible that a deviant and exciting appearance can be greeted, accepted, and fostered. Yes, given accepted understandings of reality, it may be vulgar and heretical. Yes, given limited levels of tolerance, it may be romantic and sensational. Yes, it may engender the strife and enthusiasm of commotion. But it is entertained; the aesthetic experience is had. It is had because it is just such unorthodox and interesting aspects of aesthetic experience that make it satisfying. And it is just such satisfaction that renders the aesthetic experience intrinsically valuable.

We said, at the beginning of Chapter II, that theology and religion are oriented toward that which is of intrinsic value. And we proceeded to argue that what is of intrinsic value is aesthetic experience. And now we are claiming that the result of aesthetic experience and the essence of theology and religion is commotion. In anticipation of what will follow, we can say that theology and religion oscillate around commotion because they are concerned primarily with beauty rather than with truth or ethics.

I. THEOLOGY AND TRUTH

Theology should be a particular kind of aesthetic inquiry. As a form of aesthetic inquiry, theology should present propositions which contrast with reality so that they will evoke in the reader mental appearances which contrast with his physical feelings of reality. Hence, theology should be beautiful, in that it should evoke the experience of beauty. But as a particular kind of aesthetic inquiry, theology should concentrate on the question, What is the meaning of life? As Paul Tillich has said,[1] the question of existential meaning should be the subject matter of theology. So theology should aim to present imaginative propositions about the meaning of life, propositions that advance beyond and contrast with common and accepted understandings of the meaning of life. Jesus was formulating a theological proposition when he said: "You have heard that it was said, 'You shall love your neighbor and hate your enemy.' But I say to you, Love your enemies and pray for those who persecute you." [2] Today there are popular and accepted notions that the meaning of life lies in devotion to country, to career, to family, or to one's own salvation. Theological propositions should contrast with such notions.

Theology should not be concerned primarily with truth. When it is, theology presents propositions about the meaning of life that correspond with the common and accepted cultural heritage about the meaning of life. It ferrets out those conscious or unconscious elements of belief about the meaning of life which are implicit in any culture, and it presents explicit theological propositions which accurately correspond with cultural beliefs. But we are arguing that theology should foster interpretations of meaning that aesthetically contrast with common and accepted meanings. And we have argued that to continue to expound and accept propositions which truthfully correspond to reality causes an addiction to dogmatic reiteration and, eventually, a degradation of life forms.

With an aesthetic orientation, theology can become a more disturbing enterprise than it is usually thought to be. If a theological proposal is accepted, the meaning of life is interpreted in the guise of the theological proposition—even though the heritage of accepted interpretations of the meaning of life contrasts with the theological proposition. It is the devaluation of truth and this promotion of disturbing aesthetic contrasts which would make theology a form of commotion. Theology should be a planned commotion because its propositions should contribute to intellectual commotion in the reader of theology and to enacted commotion in religion.

This is not to indicate that theology should disregard truth or that it should become merely a bastion of chaos. While theology should not be primarily oriented toward truth, it should be cognizant of truth, especially truth about common and accepted understandings of the meaning of life. Without that cognizance, an aesthetically oriented theology would become either vague or trivial, for it would be too ignorant about reality to formulate propositions that contrast with reality.

It cannot be argued that, in the past, theology has been ignorant of the truth about common and accepted understandings of the meaning of life. If anything, theology has been overly concerned with a truthful reiteration of those understandings—theology has copied secular or sacred culture all too often. Vagueness and triviality ensued, not because of a disregard for truth, but because of a preoccupation with truth.

During the early decades of the twentieth century in the United States, the movement in Protestant theology called liberalism or modernism proposed theological notions that suffered from vagueness. Liberalism was preoccupied with certain truths of secular culture. But liberalism's theological propositions were so similar to these optimistic and pseudoscientific popular views of life that there was not sufficient contrast between liberalism's theological propositions and those views of life to cause significant aesthetic reaction. Much the same could be said of the "death of God" movement in the 1960's. In some instances, its theological theory so closely corresponded with a certain accepted secular, humanistic view of life that significant contrast with that perception of life was absent. Theology suffering from vagueness in its relation to secular interpretations of meaning is burdened with the question: "What makes your proposal distinctively theological? Secular culture has said this many times before. So what else is new?"

Conservatism has been so preoccupied with truths about Christian tradition that it suffers from triviality. Conservatism's theological propositions differ so much from common and accepted secular perceptions of life that its appearance is irrelevant to secular perceptions, and significant aesthetic contrast is lost. Classical or Reformation theology, at the time of its formulation, may have proposed appearances that contrasted nicely with common and accepted views—as they were then held. But when those same theological appearances are brought into relation with life as it is commonly perceived by secularists in the twentieth century, they seem, as they say, to be without relevance. Neo-orthodoxy and fundamentalism seem to be convinced that the old message is still powerful because it presents to current secular views of life an interpretation of meaning that is radical (yes, revolutionary!). But conservatism is sometimes shoved aside with the exasperated and puzzled exclamation, That's simply incredible!

Admittedly, these assessments of liberalism and conservatism are crude generalizations. But they might indicate that a preoccupation with truth might lead to theological propositions that do not contribute to the evolution of secular culture. It seems legitimate to hope that theology might present propositions that contrast with common and accepted understandings of the meaning of life. Such propositions could contribute to present evolution by evoking appearances that contrast with reality and that therefore foster experience that is intrinsically valuable. And such propositions could contribute to the future evolution of culture by presenting it with fresh possibilities for the interpretation of the meaning of life. Of course, we are arguing that an aesthetically oriented theology is more likely to serve these functions.

The analysis cannot be terminated here, however. The relation between an aesthetically oriented theology and truth is more complex than we have indicated. We have maintained that if one is to present aesthetically significant propositions about the meaning of life, he should not be primarily concerned with truth, but he should be cognizant of truth, so that his propositions will relate to reality with contrast, rather than with vagueness or triviality. However, theology does not simply present any kind of proposition about the meaning of life. If theology is to be theological, it says that the meaning of life pertains to something ultimate, some reality which is more than simply the sum of past events. Theology calls this ultimate, God. With an aesthetic orientation similar to that described in Chapter III, a theology must acknowledge that the novelty in its propositions about the meaning of life is derived from God. That novelty is a reflection of God; it corresponds to something in God; it embodies a truth about God. This is truth of a different order; it is not the truth in the correspondence between an appearance and past actual reality. It is the truth that Whitehead refers to as "that truth-relation whereby Appearance summons up new resources of feeling from the depths of Reality." [3] To acknowledge that an aesthetically oriented theology purports to have this kind of truth in no way nullifies our claim that theological propositions should contrast with, rather than correspond to, the common and accepted meanings of life inherited from the past. In fact, it is the novel truths about God that allow theological propositions to deviate from, rather than correspond to, the common and accepted meanings of life.

When an aesthetically oriented theology claims that its propositions include truths about God, this theology acknowledges that its propositions were formulated in a moment of religious experience. This theology acknowledges that the person who formulated the theological proposition was inspired by God, in that he received from God a novelty which gave distinctiveness to the proposition. Or, it could be said that the novelty that inspires is a revelation from God. An aesthetically oriented theology should acknowledge this influence of God in the formulation of all significance and new propositions about the meaning of life—whether it is Jesus reinterpreting eschatology, Marx reinterpreting history, or Martin Luther King reinterpreting the strategies of civil rights.

It is certainly fair to ask why any discipline should

claim the influence of God in the formulation of its propositions. Theology cannot respond with a proof establishing that there is a God and that he influences the formulation of theological propositions. Theology, when it posits the existence of a God and claims that God provides men with novel ideas, is attempting simply to describe the nature of a human phenomenon. In Chapter III, we indicated why it seems to make more sense to speak of novel ideas coming from outside and hitting a person, rather than of novel ideas being conjured up out of a person's guts. In Chapter I we cited the ways in which Harvey Cox, David Miller, and Sam Keen argued that man stands receptive to the influence of God in moments of wonder and fantasy and celebration and play. Perhaps it simply adds confusion to call that source of influence God. Nevertheless I agree that novelty is received from some source beyond man. Those novelties which I experience in moments of aesthetic value are novelties *I* am not responsible for. They were given to me. And it seems satisfactory to say that there is some source for those novelties, something that has given them to me, something that *is* responsible for those novelties, something that is luring me and other creatures into moments of present satisfaction and future development.

The attitude of one who is thinking theologically has been called faith. Faith involves trust, in that it is willing to entertain seriously an appearance that deviates from reality. Faith involves absurdity because it trusts appearances that deviate from reality. To use Sören

Kierkegaard's language: "Instead of objective uncertainty there is here a certainty, namely that objectively it is absurd; and this absurdity held fast in the passion of inwardness, is faith." [4] Faith involves belief, in that it takes seriously the possibility that the novelty implicit in the appearance may say something true about God. Finally, faith involves temporary commitments, in that it chooses—for the time being, at least—to view reality in terms of appearance's interpretation. The set of attitudes of one whose orientation is aesthetically theological can be interpreted as faith. Then, faith can be viewed as aesthetic experience, in that it entertains the contrast between the proposed appearance and the given reality. Because faith can be viewed as aesthetic experience, it can be thought of as intrinsically valuable.

For example, when someone entertains and accepts a novel interpretation of the love of God, he exercises a capacity of faith, which operates in the following manner. Faith involves trust when it entertains the novel proposition that love is what is ultimate in reality. Faith includes an awareness of the absurdity of such an interpretation of a seemingly loveless world. Faith involves belief when it says that love might be related to what is ultimate in reality, or to God. And faith involves a temporary commitment when it decides to see reality in the guise of that love interpretation of reality. Faith is aesthetic experience when it feels the contrast between that appearance and reality. Faith says, What if we see reality as persuaded by love!

II. THEOLOGY AND GOODNESS

Only so long can a person keep corked that better self. After continued neglect, it begins to plot a break. It anticipates prompt arrest. But in the interim, in the transistory freedom, it can speak. It can capture a radio station. It can storm a meeting and seize the microphone. At least, it can stand up in a park and, with Bertolt Brecht, say:

Indeed I live in the dark ages!
A guileless word is an absurdity. A smooth fore-
    head betokens
A hard heart. He who laughs
Has not yet heard
The terrible tidings.

Ah, what an age it is
When to speak of trees is almost a crime
For it is a kind of silence about injustice!
And he who walks calmly across the street,
Is he not out of reach of his friends
In trouble?

It is true: I earn my living
But, believe me, it is only an accident.
Nothing that I do entitles me to eat my fill.
By chance I was spared. (If my luck leaves me
I am lost.)

They tell me: eat and drink. Be glad you have it!
But how can I eat and drink
When my food is snatched from the hungry

And my glass of water belongs to the thirsty?
And yet I eat and drink.[5]

"Babies are now dying in Brazil from starvation and malnutrition," adds the better self. "Washington generals are proposing necessary weapons for possible wars. Washington politicians are proposing nonviolence for oppressed minorities. Washington lobbyists are proposing subsidies for affluent industries. How can anyone talk of beauty in such times?" The aesthetic self is stunned. The better self continues. "You talk of beauty and peasants are killed. You talk of beauty, and you and I and the powerful and the rich are killing. You go to hell! We will burn these pages to heat cold huts. We will erase from these pages your pictures of smiles. We will cover these pages with the graffiti of those who suffer. We will wad these pages to gag the slack throats of aesthetes.

"Indeed, whenever beauty has been entertained, the ages have been dark. Beauty requires leisure, and leisure is bought by the servitude of the masses. The playground of beauty is the backs of slaves. How can one call for the luxury of beauty when his brother is still calling for food and shelter and justice? How can one be bothered by the question of intrinsic value for today when his brother is still obsessed with the instrumental value of gaining subsistence for tomorrow? Leave your library and go to the streets. To talk of beauty is not in itself evil. But in this age it is untimely, and it is a distraction with evil effects. Hold your talk of beauty until an age when justice reigns—if such an age ever comes. In our age the problem is not to sweeten the stolen leisures of the fortunate few, but to restore the human dignity of the unfortunate multitudes.

"Amen." He is caught, arrested, hauled off, recorked.

On this frail voyage, that is the voice of the siren. We will do our best to steer clear. Perhaps the reader knows better. Perhaps the voice should lure; perhaps this enterprise should shipwreck. But we are incapable of such circumspection and we shall defend our course.

The gist of our defense can be expressed in a reply to the voice of the better self: Attack beauty and aesthetes as you will; but the sensitivity and discernment of your ethical attack is still fresh from the womb of aesthetic imagination. Ethical sensitivity and discernment is a child of aesthetic sensibility Without aesthetics, ethics has no resources for a significant response. How do you presume to be the better self?

We could always refer that better self to Chapter II, where we argued that the ethical aim cannot be of intrinsic value. But the better self's objection seems unconcerned with such questions. This is not the age for pleasantries about intrinsic value; this is the age for instrumental action. If that means that the satisfaction of intrinsic value will be missed, survival warrants such sacrifice. Or we could refer the better self to Chapter III, where we argued that the ethical aim for the future must be directed toward aesthetic value: the present must be beautiful for the future so that the future can hope to attain the intrinsic satisfaction of the experience of beauty. But here we will be concerned with neither the allocation of intrinsic value nor the nature of ethical aims. Here we will be concerned with the quality of the ethical response. We will contend that particular moral responses originate from aesthetic insight. Without aesthetic insight one cannot respond to a situation with sensitivity and discernment.

In practical living the crucial ethical predicament is not that of deciding on the proper values to strive for, in the spirit of the teleologists, nor that of invoking the proper rules of conduct, in the spirit of the deontologists. Very few wars between nations or battles between persons have come about because men acted teleologically rather than deotologically, or because they were ignorant of values that condemn conflict or of laws that outlaw conflict. It was something else that went wrong. Very few minority groups have been relegated to the periphery of a society and very few strangers have been left in need because there were still a few questions of value or duty yet unsettled. The crucial factor was elsewhere.

Now Christian theorists will say, "Of course, the problem is not ignorance but a selfish will!" They will argue that man fails to do the good, not because he is ignorant of the good or the right, but because his will is directed toward his selfish satisfaction rather than toward the general welfare. They will say that if God changes man's will, then man will become more moral. Now certainly there is some merit to this classical rejoinder. Principles must be supplemented with inclination; and it is proper to sense that, when things go wrong morally, principles may not be the crucial consideration. But simply to posit a good will as the solution is inadequate.

In practical morality the skill of insight is necessary. This skill is distinct from and prerequisite to any adequate use of known values or duties or any adequate function of the will. Without this, knowledge of the good and the right is merely academic. Without this, a high-minded will can be sinister in its effects. Without this, practical morality can be a force of personality without sensitivity, a thrust of good intentions without discernment. With this skill, a particular moral response can become both sensitive, or empathetic, and discerning, or relevant.

In the parable of the good Samaritan it is not likely that the priest and the Levite passed on the other side of the road because they were ignorant of ethical principles: one must assume that they were well versed in Hebrew law. Nor is there any indication in the parable that they were afflicted with an egocentric will or had an ill will for the beaten man. What they lacked, and what the good Samaritan had, was compassion: "And when he saw him, he had compassion." (Luke 10:33.) The parable is given in answer to the question, Who is my neighbor? The priest and the Levite lacked the capacity to see and feel the beaten man as their neighbor, as one who is to be loved as one loves himself. They apparently lacked sensitivity to, or empathy for, the man. Empathy is "imaginative projection of one's own consciousness into another being." [6] Because they lacked empathy, they failed to see and feel that the beaten man was a man as they were, and thus the appropriate object of the same kind of love as the love they had for themselves. Lacking this sensitivity, they failed even to initiate a positive response to the man. Since no positive response was initiated, we have no knowledge of how discerning their response might have been.

What must have been going on in the mind of the Samaritan? Three men are walking down the road to Jericho. Two of them see a beaten man lying in the road and they pass on. One of them sees a beaten man lying in the road and he stops and cares for the man. It seems plausible to say that the last man, the Samaritan, introduced into his assessment of the scene a consideration that the first two did not. Apparently, as he approached the beaten man, the Samaritan entertained an interpretation of the man before him: What if this beaten man were viewed as my neighbor, as one who should be loved as I love myself? And, apparently, the Samaritan accepted that interpretation, and thought, Yes, I will view that man as my neighbor. So he stopped and in stopping indicated that he had decided to be sensitive to the man, to treat him with empathy. That decision was itself a moral act. But the Samaritan went on to wonder, Now that I have decided to treat this man with empathy, what should I do? This involved the consideration: What would I like to have done to me if I were lying mute and wounded and a stranger were to pass by? Would I like to view myself as in need of a good scolding about traveling the road to Jericho alone? No. Would I like to view myself as one in need of bandages and a few days in an inn for recuperation? Yes.

In short, the Samaritan brought aesthetic imagination

to the scene. He entertained possibilities about the scene that were not explicitly obvious in the scene. The beaten man had no sign on him saying, Here lies your brother! The Samaritan's initial interpretation of the scene can be understood in terms of the proposition: this man (the logical subject) can be viewed as my neighbor (the pure potential predicated of the subject). This proposition constitutes an appearance, or a way of interpreting the reality that is confronted. Now if the Samaritan had eschewed an imaginative interpretation of the scene, he would have simply and accurately thought: H'mmm. There lies a beaten man in the road. There would then have been no reason for not passing on. Instead, the Samaritan introduced a novel and propositional interpretation of the scene. This was aesthetically entertained when it was juxtaposed with the reality and felt as a contrast. This contrast could be expressed in a question: What if this real, bloody, forsaken, strange body were viewed as one who should be loved as I love myself? That constitutes a real contrast. Add to this the fact that a Samaritan in the region of Jerusalem would very likely think of a beaten stranger as an ethnic enemy. So the contrast was heightened: the stranger is an enemy stranger; and this is the reality juxtaposed with the appearance of the stranger as the loved neighbor. Our point is that it is such an aesthetic approach to the situation which made possible the empathy and sensitivity of the Samaritan. But that aesthetic approach would make possible not only an ethical sensitivity; it would make possible also a discerning and relevant ethical activity. For aesthetic imagination is also required when possible courses of action are contemplated. It is as though the Samaritan entertained certain possible ways of interpreting the need of the beaten man and contrasted such interpretations with the reality presented to him by the ailing body on the road. According to the parable, the Samaritan hit on one interpretation, aesthetically felt the contrast between that interpretation and the reality of the needful body on the road, and decided to accept that interpretation as the best interpretation of the need and thus as the way to act on that body. That interpretation, or appearance, could be expressed as a proposition: the beaten man (the logical subject) should be viewed as one in need of bandages and recuperation (the predicate).

This analysis does not indicate that an awareness of values and duties is useless. But, in particular practical moral situations, questions of values and duties are not usually what is morally problematic. The tough ethical problems do not involve debate about whether love and justice are important; both parties to a dispute will almost always acknowledge that love and justice are important. The tough ethical problems have to do with getting oneself and others to be sufficiently sensitive to realize that love and justice are demanded in a particular situation, and sufficiently discerning to realize how they should be applied in the situation. For example, the real debate over racial justice does not revolve around the question of whether one should be just to human beings. Rather, it has to do with getting the racist to be sensitive to the fact that a black is human, just as he is human, and getting him to see why the black is enraged about being treated as nonhuman. So the most effective approach to the racist is not to lecture him on justice, but to have him listen to a dramatic portrayal of what it is like to be a black in the United States.

Nor has the foregoing analysis indicated that having a proper inclination of will is unimportant. In fact, it could be argued that having a will that is egocentric can itself block sensitivity and discernment. But the crucial fact is that no matter how one might be commanded to direct his will toward the good of the neighbor, the will will never empathize with the neighbor and will seldom act most effectively for the neighbor if the individual lacks aesthetic sensitivity for him and aesthetic discernment concerning what will be good for him. It is often said that likes and dislikes cannot be commanded, but that will can be commanded.[7] But can a sensitive and discerning will be created by a command? It can be argued that contemporary indifference to the peril of overpopulation is due to an egocentric will. And there is some truth to such an assessment. But even if one were motivated by a conscientious will, one would not be able to feel the weight of the problem and act with the vigor that is required unless he could muster the imagination to feel the pain of hunger, and the anguish of parents whose children die of malnutrition. Most especially, one must have the imagination to envision other places (strange lands and peoples) and other times (the situation thirty-five years from now when world population will be doubled), and to think of how one might act to meet the problems in those places and times. An aesthetic awareness is needed to awaken the will.

This approach to the nature of ethical problems and responses emphasizes the sin of ommission—rather than the sin of commission. The heart of moral inadequacy is a failure to imagine fresh interpretations, or appearances, and to contrast these with the realities of a situation. First, there is the failure to be sensitive to the situation; usually this means that one fails to have empathy, fails to imagine what it would be like to be in the problematic situation himself. Second, there is the failure to be discerning in one's reaction to a situation; usually this means that one fails to imagine relevant active responses to the situation. The first is an imaginative act that helps one to realize *that* an ethical response is appropriate. The second is an imaginative act that helps one to realize *what* the ethical response ought to be. Each type of imagination creates an appearance that must be contrasted with reality, as an interpretation of reality.

Obviously, there are sins of commission, where wrongful activity is more obvious than a failure to act rightfully. But the importance of sins of commission is usually exaggerated because they are more sensational. We think of a few acts of violence in the ghetto, rather than the centuries of neglect that produced the ghetto. We make movies about tyrants and criminals, rather than about those who let them get away with it. And it should be noted that a good case could be made for the thesis that sins of commission arise from earlier sins of omission.

It is easy to say that United States imperialism in Southeast Asia in the 1960's is simply a manifestation of bloodthirsty aggression. But it is probably more important to say that that aggression arose from United States failure to appreciate the virulence of its sense of manifest destiny and, especially, a failure to appreciate the intricacies of Vietnam: a history of oppression, a history of resistance to oppression, the nationalistic nature of Vietnamese communism, Vietnamese antipathy toward China, the historic unity of Vietnam, the civil war status of the conflict, and a lack of Vietnamese predilection for certain Western forms of government.

To argue that sins of omission are more important than sins of commission is to hold that sloth is more dangerous than aggressiveness. For it is lazy addiction to routines and stereotypes that causes one to neglect the novelties of aesthetic appreciation. When discussing speculative reason, the function of reason which makes possible imaginative insights, Whitehead does not argue that some form of malevolent irrationality is the opposite of such reason. He says:

> "Fatigue" is the antithesis of Reason. The operations of Fatigue constitute the defeat of Reason in its primitive character of reaching after the upward trend. Fatigue means the operation of excluding the impulse towards novelty.[8]

If the ability to conceive of fresh interpretations of real situations is lost, ethical sensitivity and discernment are cut off at their source.

But would this emphasis on novelty in ethics seem to

say, The wilder the innovation and the wider the contrast between the interpretation of a situation and the reality of that situation, the better the ethical sensitivity and discernment? In Chapter III we said that one criterion for beauty could be crudely expressed in the following way: The greater the contrast between appearance (or interpretation) and reality, within the identity of a unified experience, the greater the beauty of that contrast. By such reasoning, could the Marquis de Sade become beauteous and, thus, ethically exemplary? He was innovative and he did propose interpretations of sexual practices that deviated widely from accepted and real practices. But to accept these interpretations would be to accept not only unorthodox sexual practices but also the torture, rape, and murder of innocent people that accompanied them. Could an aesthetic basis for ethical sensitivity and discernment lead to such diabolical results? What can be said of the fact that there is a strong aesthetic attraction in boxing matches, bull fights, war films, the exploits of dictators, crime stories, race car accidents, or almost any act of violence? What can be done with the fact that the first half of Malcolm X's autobiography, which moves through episodes in a criminal underworld, is more readable than the second half, which centers on Malcolm X's spiritual reform? Would an aesthetical orientation in ethics, then, call for more violence and crime?

Certainly, this could be the peril of an aesthetic orientation: it might be ethically irresponsible. Two considerations might indicate that this need not happen. First, we have argued that if appearance—the interpretation—differs too much from reality, relevance and contact with reality is lost. The result is triviality. So an excessively innovative appearance could be rejected on aesthetic grounds. Second, when we advocated an aesthetically based ethics, we were concerned with one thing only: the resources for a sensitive and discerning moral response. We were concerned with how someone gets the ideas that make it possible for him to accomplish, morally, what should be accomplished. It is as though we were describing what it takes to drive a car: the driver must be sensitive and responsive to the road, and not simply barrel ahead. We were not talking about where the car should be driven. Admittedly, if one were concerned only about the present act of skillful driving, he could just as well skillfully drive through his neighbor's backyard as he could skillfully drive down his narrow alley. But, as was noted in Chapters II and III, ethics is teleological, or consequence-oriented. For ethics, action in the present moment is subordinated to considerations concerning the next moment. So ethical sensitivity and discernment are directed, not toward aesthetic satisfaction in the present moment, but toward providing the conditions for aesthetic satisfaction in future moments. The aim of ethics is to create in the present beautiful conditions, conditions that will make most likely the experience of beauty in future moments. While this requires aesthetic resources in the present moment, the satisfaction of the present aesthetic experience of imagining contrasts is not itself the primary criterion. The primary criterion for ethics is: Will the consequences of present acts be such that future experience of beauty will be more likely? Obviously, to accept and act on diabolical interpretations of reality in the present will inhibit one's own or others' possibilities for the future experience of beauty. So they should be rejected.

However, this is not to say that the intellectual entertainment of diabolical interpretations of reality is not valuable. Perhaps teachers of sex education should read the Marquis de Sade. The experience of the contrasts between the Marquis de Sade's proposals and reality will usually be followed by the rejection of those proposals. But the experience of the contrast and the decision to reject can be morally valuable because they can make one more sensitive and discerning. Antiwar satire, presenting blood and gore, presupposes that there is moral value in experiencing and rejecting diabolical interpretations of reality.

Earlier, the voice of the better self—the self asserting the primacy of ethics—maintained that aesthetics and a concern for beauty are inappropriate in our age. We have attempted to answer this charge in part. We have argued that aesthetic awareness is not only appropriate, but indispensable, if the individual is to be sensitive and discerning in his response to a particular situation. The indignation expressed by the better self is itself a result of an aesthetic response. The better self was not simply viewing the realities of life. It was viewing those realities as they stood in contrast with ideal and imagined possibilities for life. The better self was saying: There is hunger, and there could be health. There is strife, and there could be peace. The feeling of these contrasts is what we have called an aesthetic feeling. While the better self might concede this, it might still insist that this ethical use of aesthetics—for the benefit of others in one's future—is the only legitimate use. It might still insist that any concern for one's own present aesthetic satisfaction is wrong.

Finally, there is a problem which the better self did not raise but which seems also to call for an aesthetic orientation in ethics. What can be done with the fact that often men feel they lack the freedom to do what they think they ought to do? What in Christian thought has been called "original sin" or "the bound will" seems to describe a very natural condition. In Romans, Paul said, "I do not do what I want, but I do the very thing I hate." (Rom. 7:15.) Paul is not indicating an inability to see what his ethical aim should be—he knows what he wants and hates. This agrees with our argument that basic values and duties are not in question. Rather, there is a felt inability to do in the present what ought to be done. We have argued also that this inability is not primarily an inability of will. It is an inability to be ethically sensitive and discerning. Then the question is, How can this inability be dealt with? How can the individual acquire the aesthetic resources to generate ethical sensitivity and discernment sufficient for the active pursuit of what he knows to be the proper ethical aim? And, of course, our answer is that God, as he is beautiful, as he promotes aesthetic awareness, provides those resources. But let us explain.

In Chapter III we argued that God provides the novelty that allows appearance to deviate from reality. Here we can say that it is those pure potentials presented to the subject by God which allow the subject to become ethically sensitive to the situation and ethically discerning regarding what the response to the situation should be. Then, for example, the good Samaritan can find it possible to see the beaten man as (in the appearance of) his neighbor and as one who needs succor. Without these new potentials the Samaritan would probably persist in seeing simply a body lying in the road. With these new potentials the Samaritan can interpret the situation in a way that the situation did not itself demand and in a way that the Samaritan did not in himself invent. An individual is given potentials. He stands in a receptive posture. He is given new eyes and a fresh understanding that enables him to be ethically sensitive and discerning. He is enlightened by what has traditionally been called grace. And by grace we refer to the unexpected enlightenment that occurs in all aesthetic experience and not only in what are traditionally called "religious" contexts.

Also in Chapter III we argued that God's effect on men could be called general revelation, because the locus of God's lure for novelty is uncircumscribed by any historical or geographical perimeters. Thus, potentially all men can be recipients of God's lure. How then can it be explained that most humans suffer from an inability in certain crucial situations to muster the imagination to be sensitive and discerning? It seems too simple to say that they are not open to these new potentials for interpreting the world. But that is true. And it does not help much to say that they lack faith. But that is true. However, the important question is, How does one acquire that openness and that faith?

The answer, it seems to me, lies in effective religious instruction, whether that be from the pulpit of a church, from a soapbox in a park, or from across a table in a tavern. The *data* of religious instruction would be the details of problematic situations, rather than the particulars of theories of value, duty, or will.[9] Without an intimate familiarity with the subtleties of white racism, for example, there is little possibility that one will acquire an empathetic sensitivity or a relevant discernment of whites and blacks in the United States. But the *message*, the interpretation, of religious instruction, brought to this data, would be: just as God, or the source of fresh potentials, is beautiful for you, you should be beautiful for your neighbor. Just as you have received resources for aesthetic awareness, you should give resources for aesthetic awareness to your neighbor. You should be sensitive to his needs and discerning in your response to his needs. The essence of religious instruction is: Imitate God! "Be merciful, even as your Father is merciful." (Luke 6:36.) "You, therefore, must be perfect, as your heavenly Father is perfect." (Matt. 5:48.) Now it is the hope of religious instruction that a recognition of the grace that comes to man and an exhortation to imitate that grace in dealing with one's neighbor will serve as an incitement to openness and faith. It is the hope of religious instruction that the call to imitate God can prompt one to be open to new possibilities, so that he will have the imagina-

tive capacities to help others as God has helped him. If
that incitement works, then one would try to pry himself
out of dogmatic closures, to be more tolerant of the innovations that come to him, and to be more inclined to
play speculatively with those innovations. To state it
theologically, he would be more likely to accept, through
faith, the grace of God, so that, in turn, he would have
a greater potential to become sensitive and discerning
about the good for his neighbor. This can be summarized
and supplemented by comment on a recent book.

Jerry Rubin in *Do It!* says that God is a Yippie.[10] I
say Jerry Rubin is a religious prophet.[11] Jerry Rubin is
interested in engendering social change that will make
love and community [12] more likely. But he chooses to do
this not by telling the truth, but by exaggerating.[13] He
chooses to engender social change not by speaking of
moral values, but by using techniques to get people to
act.[14] He attempts to make people sensitive to the evils
of the situation by juxtaposing, against the realities of
the situation, imaginative interpretations of those realities. He conveys these interpretations by satirical, comic,
ironic, offensive, and obscene rhetoric and by theatrical
actions.[15] He does not comment on the epistemological
source of his uncanny speculations. But he is a man who
can choose to appear, as a subpoenaed witness, before
the House Un-American Activities Committee, in a revolutionary war costume.[16] Given what we have said about
epistemological sources, it seems logical to propose that
God is the source of the innovative idea that made such
interpretations possible.

Rubin's distinctive form of social persuasion [17] contains an additional element. Rubin says that his efforts to change society are fun.[18] This conclusion supports what we have said earlier. We have said that aesthetic experience is the contrast between appearance and reality; and we have argued that this experience is intrinsically satisfying. Here we have said that Rubin is dealing in aesthetic contrasts; so it would follow that he would have fun, if by fun he means immediate satisfaction. In short, while ethics aims at creating conditions for the future experience of beauty, it deals in aesthetic contrasts and, consequently, should be satisfying in the moment of present experience.

III. THEOLOGY AND BEAUTY

The foot wriggled and drummed its toes and asked, "Would you find it fitting to accompany me on a walk before dark?"
"If it is interesting," answered the shoe.

We have said that interest exists in the experience of the contrast between appearance and reality. And this reminds me that I once attended a lecture advertised under the following title: "How to Flatulate in Public Without Embarrassment." It was in the month of March, the thirteenth lecture in a series of guest lectures in theology. The lectures were given by local ministers, on an engineering school campus. While the campus had ten thousand resident students, rarely more than ten students were in attendance at the lectures. The evening of this lecture, three hundred students stood in the hall seeking entrance to the small room where the lecture was to be given. The meeting place was changed to the largest lecture theater on campus, and within half an hour of the original starting time the lecture began in the new location. The speaker, a small man, with the rapt attention of all, delivered a rather conventional talk on the sin of hypocrisy. At the end a student rose to say: "I listened to your talk. But why the title?" The minister said: "You must develop an eructation that sounds exactly like a flatulation. Then, if you flatulate, as soon as possible, eruct. And all will think the first noise was merely the first eructation in a series of eructations." Then he himself emitted a terrific belch (or the believers contended it was a belch), and left.

You might well say, "Why spoil a nice book about God and beauty with a nasty story about . . . you know what?" And well might I answer. For, dear reader, I care little about my reputation. I am marked, and soon will be gone. Who knows? Perhaps, even as you read these words, I will have. . . . It is a terminal illness. The experts still debate whether it is hereditary; but they agree that it was there at birth. There are many who are not even conscious that it exists. It is accompanied by no sores, telltale cough, or sallow complexion. But, unlike breaking wind, there is no way to cover it up, once you yourself know you have it. I am infected with incurable, galloping mortality.

So, for my few remaining days, I will advocate the consolations of religion—where the satisfaction of the present moments, at least, can from time to time be savored, where reality can be toyed with, where boredom can sporadically be conquered.

Religion is the public activity that enacts aesthetic contrast, just as theology is the theoretical activity where aesthetic contrast is conceptually entertained and planned. Religion is the communal participation in jokes and pathos and in stories and ceremonies that comment in a fresh way on the stagnant realities of society.

The essence of religion is the contrast between the sacred and the profane. Religion is not found in a rarified sacredness; it is found in the relation between the sacred and the profane. The sacred by itself, apart from communication with the world, has the appeal of the cloistered face and the dry mouth of the monk; it has the pertinence of baroque music played on an organ in an empty church. The profane is the world apart from the sacred; and the profane, if not nerved by the sacred, is a dead, sterile, repetitive beat. The sacred and the profane are interdependent, and bring benefits to each other. The sacred brings to the present moment some new vision of how reality might be dealt with; it demands that the present at least toy with the possibility of evolution beyond the past. The profane brings reality to the present moment; it demands that the present be cognizant of the truth about the past. The public collision of the profane world and the sacred creates the public enactment of beauty. That public enactment of beauty is religion. Religion is enacted in the declaration that there shall be peace in a world that is truly at war. It is enacted in the nonviolent civil rights protest in the center of a city that is subtly, but with organization, committing violence against blacks. It is enacted in a Salvation Army solicitation in the canyons of commercial Christmas: think of the shivering bells of the Salvation Army, seeking funds for the needy, within earshot of the warm ring of the cash register, working over Christmas for the greedy. It is enacted even in the reading of the Bible and the performance of religious ritual, when these are done with an appreciation of how they contrast with the world in which they are read and performed: for to proclaim that there is purpose and order underlying a world that seems to have no purpose and no order, is to enact a contrast of beauty.

The public collision of the sacred and the profane is disturbing; religion is the public enactment of commotion. The true believer, the authentic practitioner of religion, is disturbing because he brings to reality a word or an act that is unorthodox and new to reality and yet relevant to reality. Often, he is a prophet of doom in times of complacency; or he is a prophet of hope in times of despair. As reality changes from a tone of complacency to a tone of despair, the activity of the prophet can change concomitantly. Ezekiel preaches doom before Israel falls and hope after Israel falls; and he heightens the contrast between profane reality and his sacred performance by utilizing in that performance wildly innovative visions and symbolic acts. Other Hebrew prophets were similarly contrary to popular sentiments. They were thought of as troublemakers, while the "false prophets" told the people what they wanted to hear and were well received. The members of the early Christian community, the founders of Christianity, inaugurated their gospel by announcing: What the world thinks is the death of our leader is interpreted by us as the birth of our hope! They were called fools.

Whether enacted by Hebrew prophet or early Christian, whether by Hindu or Buddhist, whether by a worker for civil rights or a member of the peace movement, whether by your next door neighbor over an evening beer or by your child as he plays, the religious act sets against the world a new possibility. We have referred to the new possibility as "sacred" because traditionally it has been acknowledged that the innovation that informs certain special events was inspired by a reality beyond the reality of ordinary past history. By contrast, ordinary past history is thought of as profane; it stands void of fresh, sacred innovation. The contrast between the sacred suggestion and the profane reality is felt with zeal, ecstasy, enthusiasm. It is useful simply for being felt; it has intrinsic value. It is a religious event.

Most contemporary advocates of profound and novel change refuse to associate themselves with what is called religion or the sacred. The "secularity" of the twentieth-century novelists, philosophers, scientists, and advocates of political and social change is virtually a cliché. Yet they act as though they are inspired with insights that are engendered by more than a simple working over of the past or a sheer autonomous cerebration. Given the Whiteheadian epistemology with which we are working, it seems that their innovation would be engendered somehow externally, by some lure for novelty.

Perhaps these secularist creators refuse to be associated with religion because of what they see in most contemporary institutional religion. These people are attracted by novelty, but they seldom find it in organized religion. In the machinations of organized religions, the novelty and aesthetic contrast appropriate to religious acts is usually lost in vagueness or triviality. When it is functioning properly, religion will propose as the sacred a novelty relevant to the profane world, and religion will enact the aesthetic contrast between the sacred so conceived and the profane, which is the world as it is physically and commonly received. Here it may be obvious that the sacred is correlative to what Whitehead calls appearance, and the profane is correlative to what Whitehead calls reality. The sacred is an appearance because it is a symbol in terms of which the meaning of reality is posited, or a proposition in terms of which a theoretical suggestion about reality is made. The profane is reality because it is that heritage of thought or action physically received by the subject. If religion is to avoid vagueness, its sacred appearance must be sufficiently diverse from profane reality. And if religion is to avoid triviality, its sacred appearance must be sufficiently true to the profane world.

It could be argued that most of what goes on in Christian churches is both vague and trivial. Knowing that vagueness results when the (sacred) appearance is excessively similar to the (profane) reality, and that triviality results when the appearance is excessively diverse from reality, you could well ask, "How can anything be simultaneously vague and trivial?" Of course, no appearance could be simultaneously vague and trivial with regard to the same aspect of, or data from, reality. But it can be both vague and trivial with regard to different aspects of reality. Often, the interpretations of conservative Christian religion will be vague with regard to a particular reality—the heritage of orthodox religious literature and tradition. Conservatism says that the sacred should rather closely conform to the reality of the religious literature and tradition, as it is physically received by the subject. Contrast between appearance and reality is discouraged; truth, or an identity between sacred appearance and the essence of the religious heritage, is encouraged. When conservatism attains a rough conformity between its interpretations and certain factors in the religious heritage, vagueness results. The vagueness of conservatism leads to an interesting conclusion. We have called the past, as it is physically received in the present, the profane. Because conservatism emphasizes the authority of the heritage of past religious reality, and because it demands that the sacred appearance conform closely with that past reality, conservatism promotes profanity. On the other hand, and at the same time, conservatism can be trivial with regard to the secular reality of the contemporary world. When conservatism continues to use forms of expression and rituals that were designed to address a world centuries in the past, it can become trivial for a new world. Such conservatism can present a sacred that deviates so widely from the presently experienced world, that it seems silly. Conservatism can be so cavalier and disregarding of the truth of the science, philosophy, and culture of the contemporary secular world that it loses relevance to that world and from the standpoint of that world seems incomprehensible and trivial. This duality of vagueness and triviality is often present in Protestant neo-orthodoxy.

A converse duality of vagueness and triviality can inhere in certain forms of liberalism. Liberalism's sacred appearance can deviate so widely from the Biblical and traditional Christian past that it loses contact with those realities and becomes trivial with respect to them. Liberalism becomes thin and abstract when it cuts people off from their thick, concrete religious heritage. At the same time liberalism's sacred appearance can correspond so closely with contemporary secular interpretations of reality that it becomes vague with respect to them.

For many, institutional religion still evokes an aesthetic contrast between the sacred and the profane. Aesthetic judgments are relative because they depend on how the particular subject has received reality: through the eyes of one who is black or Caucasian, male or female, educated or noneducated; and in an environment which is urban or rural, chaotic or placid, continuous or fragmented, cruel or kind. Continuous exposure to a particular environment of reality would give a particular subject a particular understanding of profane reality. For one person, a religious practice might evoke a sacred appearance that contrasts vitally with profane reality as he knows it. For another, that same religious practice might evoke a sacred appearance that relates to profane reality, as he knows it, with vagueness or triviality. "The Old Rugged Cross" and "Rock of Ages" can induce a sacred appearance that does contrast, without vagueness or triviality, to profane reality as some people know it. For others, flowing vestments, incense, and the music of Bach might evoke an aesthetically significant contrast.

But for me, as I know profane reality, the sacred appearances evoked by the church are predominantly vague and trivial. The church is for me . . . DEFUNCT! William Hamilton, the lyrical "death of God" theologian, says:

> One can choose his own language here: the theologian does not and cannot go to church, he is not interested, he is alienated (for a tenser word), he must live outside. He is not thereby a happier man, nor is he a troubled one.[19]

When I was younger, going to church could ruin my whole Sunday—but not usually my whole week. On Sundays I felt gray and sluggish. Contrary to Mr. Hamilton, I must say that living outside the church has made me a happier man. Institutional religion, as I have known it, has usually shrouded me in the boredom of vagueness or it has misfired by suggesting a sacredness that never made contact with contemporary reality as I knew it. I went seeking inspiration and stimulation and left tired and dried up. I do not think that the clergy or the church leadership are sinister. They simply failed to present novelties relevant to reality as I knew it. And their recent efforts at reform—outside of a few moves for peace and racial justice—seem petty and inadequate.

The particular practices of institutional religion have failed to present me with commotion. For example, church music, if it were to work for me, would encourage a symbolic appearance of order that diverges from and yet is relevant to the disorder that I experience in the reality of everyday life. But church music does not do this for me. With reference to the reality of everyday experience, church music seems trivial. Either that music presents a rationalistic comment that seems like a voice from the never-never land, or it drips with the emotion that most abandon along with adolescence. On the other hand, with reference to the reality I have known in the church, church music is vague. Any particular performance or composition of church music is similar to past performances and compositions. I have learned to hate organs and choirs. Church music evolves very slowly. The symbolic appearance induced by church music deviates only slightly from the reality of other church music I have experienced. It is vague and boring. I find much the same duality of triviality and vagueness in the symbolic reference induced by church decor, the mannerisms of people in a church, the vestments of the clergy, and the ceremony of church services. Often these induce a formal feeling that is irrelevant to the world and monotonously like feelings on other Sundays in other churches.

If religion is enacted commotion, caused by a collision of the sacred and the profane, how can religion present commotion to those who do not now find it in the church? Religion to be effective must be beautiful. It must be an enactment that will manifest a public intersection between the sacred and the profane and thereby encourage a private contrast between the sacred and the profane in the present experience of the observer. Religion should be received by the subject as part of his reality; but it should be a part of reality that will incite in the experience of the subject an appearance which contrasts with reality. What if there were some churches that did this?

What if there were new music in churches and a variety of music? What if hopeful music were sung in times of tragedy and tragic music were sung in times of hope? What if jazz Masses really caught on? What if ministers strolled the aisles? What if sanctuaries were abandoned? What if some churches were institutions dedicated to keeping people off balance, rather than enclaves of security? What if some churches were institutions directed toward shaking people's confidence in past dogma, rather than academies for indoctrination? What if some churches were one place where one could expect novel acts and ideas, rather than the one place safe for frightened, insecure people? What if the greatest danger in going to some churches were not falling asleep but getting overwrought?

What if seminaries taught young divines the techniques of aesthetic stimulation? What if one day we were to learn the art of causing beauty as we now know the technique of the search for truth, the means for bringing about desirable moral results, or the devices of advertising? What if we were to learn exactly what makes a story exciting or a joke funny or a conversation lively or a physical act provocative? The greatest obstacle to such an understanding is our ignorance of our initial physical feelings of reality. Usually the character of reality, that one contrasts with appearance, is unconscious. But what if we were to learn enough about the phenomenology of common physical feelings of reality to build aesthetically provocative religious enactments?

What if some churches were to find a new Christ? It may be true, as one of the Beatles said, that for many people the Beatles were more popular than was Jesus. For these people the Beatles may have presented relevant novelties that contrasted more significantly with reality than Jesus' message did. Does this mean that for these people and for other groups of people Jesus no longer embodies the relevant novelty that the sacred should present? Is Jesus no longer sacred?

Why not then seek a new Christ,[20] who can bring, in acts and words, a message that will evoke in modern secular man an appearance that will contrast with reality? Why not look to Mahatma Gandhi or Che Guevara, Martin Luther King or Malcolm X, as sacred, as Jesus was once looked to as sacred? But such suggestions never seem to ring true. Why do such suggestions always seem purely hypothetical? Is it that the mass of people are relatively ignorant of such men, so that they cannot naturally look to them as embodying a message for them? It it because such men seem more like specialists in techniques of social change or political ideology, than embodiments of a way of life? Would it seem phony to preach Che Guevara as the new Christ, because we all assume that a Christ is the savior figure in a culture, and he must be a central character with broad significance in an old cultural heritage?

But if a Christ is the savior figure of a culture and if he must be a central character with broad significance in that culture, does that imply a redefinition of what it is that makes someone a Christ for a culture? Certainly, Jesus, in the first century, embodied, and other heroes today embody a relevant novelty that allows the observer to view them as presenting something sacred. But is a Christ figure an embodiment of the sacred? Is that how a Christ figure is used in a culture? Or, if a Christ is a central character with broad significance in an old cultural heritage, is a Christ really an embodiment of something profane? Does a Christ really function as a presentation out of the past of a common and accepted way of life or meaning of life?

If a Christ functions as something profane, as part of the physically received common and accepted heritage, then the sacred is the relevant novelty that is proposed now and that is designed to contrast with the profane reality, which includes the Christ. When something profound happens in Christian theology or religion, it is not simply a true and accurate re-presentation of Jesus. Rather, it comes about as a fresh, contemporary suggestion. But that suggestion does not exist in a vacuum. It is contrasted, as a relevant novelty, to the common and accepted understanding of Jesus. It is contrasted as the sacred, as we have defined the sacred, is contrasted to the profane, as Jesus is part of the profane reality.

We are arguing that Jesus functions in our culture as something profane. In the Western world Jesus is the best known embodiment of the meaning of life. He is so well known that almost anywhere in the West it can be assumed that a general reference to him will be understood. Also, Jesus is not viewed as a specialist, but as an embodiment of a way of life, an embodiment of the meaning of life. Because he has broad significance, as an embodiment of a way of life, he can be relevant to many diverse sacred interpretations of the meaning of life.

Jesus functions as the profane base point, the given understanding, to which many novel cultural suggestions are contrasted. Many great cultural creations of the West can be seen either as a denial of or as a reinterpretation of the way of life embodied in Jesus. We will not argue that for people growing up in a Christian culture all relevant novelties, all sacred appearances, directly contrast with Jesus. There are relevant novelties that come from philosophy, science, and other secular enterprises, that have little relevance to Christ. But we are claiming that the picture of life given by Jesus still figures centrally in the cultural heritage from the past. This is what allows people still to call Jesus the Christ, and not be clearly in error; this is what allows people to call much of the Western world basically Christian, and not be clearly in error.

However, while significant contrasts between sacred appearances and the profane quality of the heritage of Jesus have been frequently enacted in secular culture, they are seldom enacted in church. I have seldom heard Martin

Luther King's interpretation of Jesus, as one who calls for civil rights, in the church; I have seldom heard Rudolf Bultmann's interpretation of Jesus, as one who gives authentic existence, in the church; I did not hear Nietzche's interpretation of Jesus, as one whose values should be transvalued, in the church; I did not hear Tolstoy's interpretation of Jesus, as one who calls for pacifism, in the church. Nor have I often heard the call for peace, as a call that might be relevant to Jesus, enunciated in the church. Nor did I see, hear, or witness art films, new political ideals, new forms of living together, as creations that might be relevant to Jesus, in the church. What if the church were to become Christian in the sense that Jesus would be viewed as the common and accepted profanity from the past, over against which every relevant novelty, every sacred appearance, might be placed in order to evoke commotion? If this request is too strenuous, why not begin to search for a new Christ?

It is hoped that one day there will be a church for many people who feel excluded from the church today. I refer to people for whom Jesus may still function, consciously or unconsciously, as the central determinant in their inherited view of life. But I also refer to people who experience chaos and absurdity in reality and want to hear novel suggestions relevant to that chaos and absurdity. I refer to people who think that culture must evolve and who want to participate in an institution that will foster that evolution. I refer to people who want the intrinsic satisfaction of participating in the commotion that arises where the sacred collides with the profane heritage of the past.

But for the time being, I, for one, will get my religion, my experience of the collision of the sacred and the profane, in coffee shops with co-workers, in taverns over a few beers with friends, from music, art, and television, in demonstration lines and political campaigns, and in the classroom and at home.

Yes, I do believe in the grace of God and in salvation, as I have attempted to characterize them. How else can I explain the innovations that have come to others and to myself except by affirming that there is an active lure, placing fresh and relevant possibilities before the inquisitive individual? These come to the individual as possibilities that he did not create. They are felt as a persuasion to move beyond reality as it has been received. They, and they alone, make possible an appearance that can deviate from and contrast with reality. The gratitude one feels as he receives these possibilities can prompt him to call the appearance animated by these possibilities the manifestation of the sacred, and to think of the gift of the appearance as gracious. The world apart from such manifestations can seem profane. It is the experience of the contrast between the sacred and the profane that can save men from the meaninglessness of a life that never has experience that is useful in itself. It is this experience that makes life worth living, that saves one from the tedium of pure truth and the frustration of pure morality. To me that experience is salvation.

EPILOGUE

Of course, the final rejoinder *is* death. All those precious, private present experiences of beauty die in turn with the perishing of each moment. And even the vapid memory of those moments and even the chance to have new moments, permanently perishes with your body's death. Then where is your religious experience, your intrinsic value? Gone forever. Without so much as a reverberating, "Amen." A flash in the night.

Beauty must then cede its independent wealth to morality—or die glamorously and tragically. Time may be atomic, but continuity still haunts. Present experience is alone actual, but future potentiality is a promise worth the birthright. Beauty must aspire to be beautiful for the future. That is its moral worth. To avoid tragedy, beauty seeks, egocentrically, to become altruistic. This moment, beauty has heightened intensity and awareness; through time, that will perish unless it is utilized for sensitivity and discernment for the future. Beauty has advanced beyond the past; that advance will be forgotten and useless unless care is taken for its implementation.

Beauty is love for life as it is felt now. But with time it can become apparent that the present atomic moment is merely an atomic part of a larger organism. The pain of death is mitigated when primary importance shifts from one's own life in the present to the life of the organism that moves on after one's death. With time, one can become aware that the 10,000 humans who die from starvation and malnutrition today are part of that organism too. Their chance for the intrinsic value of aesthetic experience went with their shriveled or bloated expiration. With time, beauty can aspire to help, to be beautiful, as God has been beautiful. Beauty can be directed, also, to love for future life.

This emphasis contrasts with all we have said. Perhaps we are left with the aesthetic appreciation of that contrast.

NOTES

CHAPTER I. SOMETHING NEW

1. M. Conrad Hyers, review of *In Praise of Play: Toward a Psychology of Religion* by Robert E. Neale, *The Christian Century*, April 1, 1970, pp. 389–390.

2. Harvey Cox, *The Feast of Fools: A Theological Essay on Festivity and Fantasy* (Harvard University Press, 1969), p. 3.

3. *Ibid.*, p. 46.

4. *Ibid.*, p. 133.

5. *Ibid.*, p. 139.

6. *Ibid.*, p. 140.

7. David L. Miller, *Gods and Games: Toward a Theology of Play* (The World Publishing Company, 1969), p. 137.

8. *Ibid.*, p. 154, quoting Joachim Wach, *The Comparative Study of Religions* (Columbia University Press, 1961), p. 65.

9. Miller, *op. cit.*, p. 168.

10. Miller acknowledges that these distinctions—religious, magical, and profane—are derived from Robert E. Neale, "Religion and Play," *Crossroads*, July–Sept., 1967.

11. Miller, *op. cit.*, p. 5.

12. *Ibid.*, p. 6.

13. *Ibid.*, p. 99.

14. *Ibid.*, pp. 170–171.

15. Robert E. Neale, *In Praise of Play: Toward a Psychology of Religion* (Harper & Row, Publishers, Inc., 1969), pp. 11–12.

16. *Ibid.*, p. 15; see also p. 19.

17. *Ibid.*, pp. 176–177.

18. *Ibid.*, p. 23.

19. *Ibid.*, p. 24.

20. *Ibid.*, p. 97; see also pp. 87, 104, 110, 121.

21. *Ibid.*, p. 126.

22. Neale, near the end of his book, says, "We have made no attempt to suggest a specifically Christian doctrine of play." *Ibid.*, p. 176.

23. See *ibid.*, p. 144.

24. See *ibid.*, p. 135.

25. See *ibid.*, Ch. 4.

26. Sam Keen, *Apology for Wonder* (Harper & Row, Publishers, Inc., 1969), p. 192.

27. *Ibid.*, p. 209.

28. *Ibid.*, p. 211.

29. Sam Keen, *To a Dancing God* (Harper & Row, Publishers, Inc., 1970), p. 5.

30. *Ibid.*, pp. 143–144.

31. *Ibid.*, p. 156.

32. Cox, *op. cit.*, p. 28.

33. Miller, *op. cit.*, p. 116.

34. Neale, *op. cit.*, p. 121.

35. Keen, *Apology for Wonder*, p. 80.

36. Cox, *op. cit.*, p. 5.

37. Keen, *Apology for Wonder*, p. 30.

38. To this and to statements concerning God that follow, Neale's argument is probably an exception, for he does not argue for a deity beyond man.

39. Neale, *op. cit.*, p. 144.

40. Miller, *op. cit.*, p. 153.

41. See Keen, *Apology for Wonder*, pp. 35 ff. and 201 ff.

CHAPTER II. THE PRIMACY OF BEAUTY

1. One exception might be Sam Keen in *Apology for Wonder*, when he calls for the timely man who will appreciate in the opportune moments both the Apollonian and Dionysian ways. If the Dionysian way is that of the aesthetic perspective, then it can be said that Keen calls, not for the primacy of the aesthetic, but for the equality of the aesthetic (or Dionysian)perspective with the Apollonian. However, in that book his attention is concentrated on the aesthetic, and in *To a Dancing God* the aesthetic seems to attain a clearly paramount position.

2. Paul Tillich, *Dynamics of Faith* (Harper & Brothers, 1958), pp. 1–4.

3. Friedrich Schleiermacher, *The Christian Faith* (Edinburgh: T. & T. Clark, 1960), pp. 12 ff.

4. Martin Luther, "The Large Catechism of Dr. Luther," *The Book of Concord* (Concordia Publishing House, 1922), p. 169.

5. John 3:18–19. Of course, this drawing of a parallel between Paul and John is made with a recognition of the great differences in the preconditions and consequences of these assertions as they are set in Romans and John.

6. Schleiermacher, *op. cit.*, p. 9.

7. Immanuel Kant, *Fundamental Principles of the Metaphysic of Morals*, in *Great Books of the Western World*, Robert M. Hutchins, ed. (Encyclopaedia Britannica, Inc., 1952), Vol. 42, p. 256.

8. *Ibid.*, p. 258.

9. *Ibid.*, p. 260.

10. John Stuart Mill, *Utilitarianism, Liberty and Representative Government* (E. P. Dutton and Co., Inc., 1951), p. 5.

11. Immanuel Kant, *The Critique of Practical Reason*, in *Great Books of the Western World*, Vol. 42, pp. 344–348.

12. Plato, *The Republic*, Book II, tr. by Benjamin Jowett (Random House), p. 44.

13. *Ibid.*, p. 45.

14. Rudolf Bultmann, *Jesus and the Word* (Charles Scribner's Sons, 1958), p. 110.

15. *Ibid.*, pp. 79–80.

16. Emil Brunner, *The Divine Imperative* (The Westminster Press, 1947), p. 114.

17. Jaroslav Pelikan, *Fools for Christ* (Fortress Press, 1955).

18. Rudolf Otto, *The Idea of the Holy* (Oxford University Press, 1958), p. 8.

19. Mircea Eliade, *The Sacred and the Profane* (Harper & Row, Publishers, Inc., 1959), p. 203.

20. Otto, *The Idea of the Holy*, p. 2.

21. *Ibid.*, p. 5.

22. Eliade, *op. cit.*, p. 10.

23. *Ibid.*

24. *Ibid.*, p. 11.

25. For this terminology, the postponement of satisfaction by work toward a "future state" applies to what we have called minimalist ethics, teleological ethics and one interpretation of deontological ethics. However, the orientation toward a "remote reality" has reference not only to the holy, as we have discussed it, but also to the Christian ethical orientation toward a remote will of God demanding subservient obedience.

CHAPTER III. A RATIONALE FOR BEAUTY

1. Heraclitus, "Fragments," in Philip Wheelwright (ed.), *The Presocratics* (The Odyssey Press, Inc., 1966), p. 71.

2. Parmenides, "Fragments," Wheelwright, *op. cit.*, p. 97.

3. Raphael Demos, "Introduction," in Raphael Demos (ed.), *Plato Selections* (Charles Scribner's Sons, 1955), p. xiii.

4. Alfred North Whitehead, *Process and Reality* (Harper & Row, Publishers, Inc., 1957), p. 317.

5. *Ibid.*, p. 318.

6. *Ibid.*

7. Alfred North Whitehead, *Adventures of Ideas* (The

Free Press of Glencoe, Inc., 1961), p. 276.

8. Whitehead, *Process and Reality*, p. 35.

9. *Ibid.*, p. 31.

10. Alfred North Whitehead, *Science and the Modern World* (New American Library, 1962), p. 115.

11. *Ibid.*, p. 101n.

12. Parmenides, "Fragments," Wheelwright, *op. cit.*, p. 97.

13. Alfred North Whitehead, *Modes of Thought* (Capricorn Books, 1958), p. 149.

14. There are similarities between this definition of beauty and the working definitions of the aesthetic suggested by Dadaism. See Robert Motherwell (ed.), *The Dada Painters and Poets* (Wittenborn, Schultz, Inc., 1951).

15. Whitehead, *Adventures of Ideas*, p. 267.

16. *Ibid.*, p. 269.

17. *Ibid.*, p. 258.

18. *Ibid.*, p. 245.

19. Here we are referring primarily to the immediately past realities, which are the objects emitting light and sound waves on the stage at the light show. However, it cannot be denied that realities in the more remote past, as their effects are passed on through memory, also cause the appearance. Some former experience wih musical performance is needed to make possible the interpretation that instruments can be played, for example. Or, in the earlier discussion of the newspaper in the panorama, it must be acquired from memory that the newspaper is a human artifact.

20. The notion that appearance and reality are associated with sense perception is taken from Alfred North Whitehead, *Adventures of Ideas*. The notion that sense perception is a form of symbolism is taken from his *Process and Reality* and from his *Symbolism* (Capricorn Books, 1959).

21. Whitehead, *Adventures of Ideas*, p. 248.

22. Whitehead discusses the nationalistic usage of symbolism in *Adventures of Ideas*, p. 249, and in *Symbolism*, Ch. 3.

23. Whitehead, *Process and Reality*, p. 392.

24. While the above description of propositions and the

aesthetic reactions to feelings of propositions is based on Whitehead's descriptions, it is very simplified, devoid of Whitehead's technical terminology. In some instances (especially, our notion that physical feelings of reality include common interpretations, or propositions, about reality) it supplements or diverges from Whitehead's descriptions. For Whitehead's theory of propositions see *Process and Reality*, Pt. II, Ch. IX and Pt. III, Ch. IV.

25. Whitehead says, "Propositions, like everything else except experience, in its own immediacy, only exist as entertained in experience." (*Adventures of Ideas*, p. 245.)

26. We do not mean to indicate that Aiken's proposition was a basic reason—by any means—for the national change of sentiment that occurred in ensuing years.

27. Whitehead, *Adventures of Ideas*, p. 270.

28. *Ibid.*, pp. 266–267.

29. *Ibid.*, p. 255.

30. Whitehead, *Process and Reality*, p. 170.

31. *Ibid.*, p. 170.

32. *Ibid.*, p. 427.

33. Whitehead refers to this as "Intensity Proper" in *Adventures of Ideas*, p. 253. See also, *ibid.*, p. 264.

34. Whitehead, *Process and Reality*, p. 41.

35. Alfred North Whitehead, *The Function of Reason* (Beacon Press, 1959), p. 8.

36. *Ibid.*, p. 89.

37. Whitehead, *Adventures of Ideas*, p. 274.

38. *Ibid.*, p. 279.

39. *Ibid.*, p. 269.

40. *Ibid.*, p. 268.

41. *Ibid.*, p. 265.

42. *Ibid.*, p. 266.

43. See *ibid.*, p. 244.

44. *Ibid.*, p. 257.

45. *Ibid.*

46. Whitehead, *Process and Reality*, p. 281.

47. Whitehead, *Adventures of Ideas*, pp. 265–266.

48. Alfred North Whitehead, *Religion in the Making* (The World Publishing Co., 1961), pp. 66–69.

49. Whitehead calls this "transmutation." See *Process and Reality*, p. 40.

50. *Ibid.*

51. *Ibid.*, pp. 381, 424.

52. Whitehead, *Adventures of Ideas*, pp. 266–267.

53. Whitehead, *Process and Reality*, p. 377.

54. See *ibid.*, p. 134.

55. *Ibid.*, p. 521.

56. *Ibid.*, p. 522.

57. Whitehead, *Religion in the Making*, p. 101.

58. *Ibid.*, p. 96.

59. What Whitehead calls the "initial aim" is also a feeling of the superjective nature of God. The initial aim gives to the newly forming subject a standpoint, a basis for gaining some perspective on the multiplicity in its past. However, since the initial aim is simply a subject's standpoint for its view of reality, it does not in itself substantially contribute to novelty in appearance or to aesthetic contrast.

60. However, a certain experience of God, at a certain moment in history, or a certain kind of experience of God, at any moment in history, might still be designated by a culture to be of ultimate significance *for* (relative to) it. That phenomenon encourages a notion of special revelation. As long as that is understood relativistically, it is consistent with the foregoing; unfortunately, Christianity and most other world religions absolutize and finalize their special revelation.

61. See John B. Cobb, Jr., *The Structure of Christian Existence* (The Westminster Press, 1967), esp. Ch. 12; John B. Cobb, Jr., "The Finality of Christ in a Whiteheadian Perspective," in Dow Kirkpatrick (ed.), *The Finality of Christ* (Abingdon Press, 1966); Schubert Ogden, *Christ Without Myth* (Harper & Row, Publishers, Inc., 1961), esp. the use of "decisive" on p. 153 and "definitive" on p. 161; and Schubert Ogden, *The Reality of God* (Harper & Row, Publishers, Inc., 1966), esp. p. 184.

62. Hartshorne's consuming interest is in rational and formal possibilities rather than in historical particularities. See esp. Charles Hartshorne, *Man's Vision of God* (Archon

Books, 1964), Ch. 1; Charles Hartshorne and William L. Reese, *Philosophers Speak of God* (The University of Chicago Press, 1963), "Introduction."

63. See the following books by Bernard E. Meland: *Modern Man's Worship* (Harper & Brothers, 1934); *Seeds of Redemption* (The Macmillan Company, 1947); *Reawakening of Christian Faith* (The Macmillan Company, 1949), soon to be reprinted by Books for Libraries, Freeport, N.Y.; *Higher Education and the Human Spirit* (The University of Chicago Press, 1953); *Faith and Culture* (Oxford University Press, 1953); and *The Realities of Faith* (Oxford University Press, 1962).

64. Stanley R. Hopper, "Whitehead: *Redivivus* or *Absconditus?*" in William A. Beardslee (ed.), *America and the Future of Theology* (The Westminster Press, 1967), pp. 112–126.

65. Donald W. Sherburne, *A Whiteheadian Aesthetic* (Yale University Press, 1961), pp. 5, 204.

66. Whitehead, *Adventures of Ideas*, p. 265.

67. *Ibid.*, p. 267.

68. *Ibid.*, p. 271.

69. Sherburne, *op. cit.*, p. 102.

70. *Ibid.*

71. It also seems crucial in the accounts of F. David Martin, "The Power of Music in Whitehead's Theory of Perception," *The Journal of Aesthetics and Art Criticism*, Vol. XXV, No. 3 (Spring 1967), pp. 313–322; and Eva Schaper, "Aesthetic Perception," *The Relevance of Whitehead* (The Macmillan Company, 1961), pp. 263–285.

72. Sherburne, *op. cit.*, pp. 163, 168. More precisely, propositions as formed by what Whitehead calls transmutation and by what Sherburne refers to as vertical transmutation would fail in this respect.

73. John B. Cobb, Jr., "Toward Clarity in Aesthetics," *Philosophy and Phenomenological Research*, 18 (1957), pp. 169–189.

74. *Ibid.*, p. 169.

75. *Ibid.*, p. 172.

76. In addition to the articles by Martin and Schaper

cited in note 71, above, Whitehead's aesthetics are analyzed by Bertram Morris in "The Art-Process and the Aesthetic Fact in Whitehead's Philosophy," in Paul Arthur Schilpp (ed.), *The Philosophy of Alfred North Whitehead* (Northwestern University, 1941), pp. 461–486; in a dissertation by John Charles Yeager, "The Primacy of Aesthetic Experience in Whitehead" (M.A. diss., Union Theological Seminary, Columbia University); and in Mary Wyman, *The Lure for Feeling* (Philosophical Library, 1960). The author is aware that these comments on relevant scholarship, as well as the preceding discussion of Whitehead, are selective and arbitrary in several respects. Only a few of Whitehead's ideas are discussed here, only one of several approaches to Whitehead's system is taken, and many questions are raised but not resolved.

CHAPTER IV. A THEOLOGY OF BEAUTY

1. Paul Tillich, *Systematic Theology*, Vol. I (The University of Chicago Press, 1956), p. 22.

2. Matt. 5:43–44.

3. Whitehead, *Adventures of Ideas*, pp. 266–267.

4. Sören Kierkegaard, *Concluding Unscientific Postscript*, tr. by David F. Swenson and Walter Lowrie (Princeton University Press, 1960), p. 188.

5. From "To Posterity," in Bertolt Brecht, *Selected Poems*, tr. by H. R. Hays (Harcourt Brace Jovanovich, 1947), p. 173. Copyright © 1947 by Bertolt Brecht and H. R. Hays. Used by permission of Harcourt Brace Jovanovich, Inc., publishers, owners of U.S. and Canadian rights; by permission of Ann Elmo Agency, Inc., owners of British Commonwealth rights.

6. *Webster's New Collegiate Dictionary* (G. & C. Merriam Company, 1958).

7. E.g., Joseph Fletcher, *Situation Ethics* (The Westminster Press, 1966), p. 106.

8. Alfred North Whitehead, *The Function of Reason* (Beacon Press, 1959), p. 23.

9. At this point in particular, but in several other ways

also, our proposal for a religious ethic is similar to that of H. Richard Niebuhr in *The Responsible Self* (Harper & Row, Publishers, Inc., 1963). Niebuhr advocates an ethical approach that begins neither with the teleologist's question, What is my goal? nor with the deontologist's question, What is the law? Rather Niebuhr would begin by asking, What is going on? and, then, What is the fitting response? There is in Niebuhr and in situation ethics in general a great reliance on man's ability to be sensitive to what is going on and to be discerning with regard to what is the fitting response. However, I am not aware that there has been explicit attention to what kind of human facility such abilities presuppose. Of course, we are contending that this facility is an aesthetic facility.

10. Jerry Rubin, *Do It!* (Simon and Schuster, 1970), p. 112.

11. This is not so surprising. Think of the visionary interpretations of the nature and destiny of Israel offered by Jeremiah. Think of Saul dancing ecstatically with a roving band of prophets. But think most especially of Ezekiel. He pictures Israel as a newborn infant, whose navel cord is not cut, who is unwashed, and who lies in an open field weltering in her blood (Ezek., ch. 16). Ezekiel did not let his hair grow, but shaved it and did things with his hair to symbolize the fate of Israel (Ezek., ch. 5). In a public place he lay on one side for 390 days and on the other 40 days, to signify the durations of Israel's and Judah's exile. He dug holes in walls and danced with a sword, all to make Israel ethically sensitive to her predicament through theatrical actions.

12. Rubin, *Do It!* p. 125.

13. *Ibid.*, p. 37.

14. *Ibid.*, p. 252.

15. See, e.g., *ibid.*, pp. 55, 58–59, 83.

16. *Ibid.*, Ch. 11.

17. If social persuasion involves both ethical sensitivity and ethical discernment, I am much more impressed with Rubin's effectiveness at engendering sensitivity than with his discernment. To say that the discerning response is revolution and anarchy is politically naïve. Perhaps his talk of

revolution and anarchy is simply a subtle "put-on."

18. See, e.g., *ibid.*, p. 37.

19. William Hamilton, "Thursday's Child," in Thomas J. J. Altizer and William Hamilton, *Radical Theology and the Death of God* (The Bobbs-Merrill Company, Inc., 1966), p. 88.

20. This question is pursued at length in Gustave H. Todrank, *The Secular Search for a New Christ* (The Westminster Press, 1969).